mini
London

The Essential **Visitors'** Guide

London mini Explorer
ISBN 10 976-8182-97-0
ISBN 13 978-976-8182-97-5

Copyright © Explorer Group Ltd 2007
All rights reserved.

All maps © Explorer Group Ltd 2007

Front cover photograph – Victor Romero

Printed and bound by
Emirates Printing Press, Dubai, UAE

Explorer Publishing & Distribution
PO Box 34275, Zomorrodah Building,
Za'abeel Rd, Dubai , United Arab Emirates
Phone (+971 4) 335 3520 **Fax** (+971 4) 335 3529
Email Info@Explorer-Publishing.com
Web www.Explorer-Publishing.com

Introduction

London is a city of contradictions – between old and new, luxury and bohemian, sprawling parks and towering structures, historical scenes and modern architecture. It is quite possibly the most wonderfully confusing place on earth. You'll find all of these and everything in between in the following pages. From the team who bought you the London Explorer Residents' Guide, the most comprehensive guide to living in this spectacular city, this mini marvel brings you the very best of both sides of London.

The Explorer Team

Contents

Overview

The Essential City

This is where old world charm and burgeoning skylines combine to create a unique character. It's the capital with a cultural mix as diverse and impressive as its many attractions. Welcome to London.

People who live in London would argue that the city is not entirely representative of the rest of England – that it's more of an entity unto itself. It's understandable – the 21st century London is a vibrant, multicultural metropolis with an enviable infrastructure, and it has more in common with New York all the way over the Atlantic than it does with York, a city just 280km up the road.

Scratch the surface a little, however, and it quickly becomes apparent that this 'new' London is merely an extension that sits comfortably alongside, without overshadowing, the old. 'Old' London is the home of Big Ben and Piccadilly Circus, the royal family and red double-decker buses. But it is also a heritage that stretches back over thousands of years, with a history that incorporates groundbreaking architecture, literary masterminds, the black plague, anti-government plots, raging fires, great sporting achievements, war, rapid expansion and world domination.

This colourful history is one of the most powerful attractions about London, and a primary reason why this essential city is at the top of so many travellers' to-do lists.

However, the powerful iconography of the cityscape is also to be thanked for capturing the imagination of hundreds of thousands of visitors each year. From the pomp of Buckingham Palace to the ceremony of the Houses of Parliament, there's plenty to fuel the stereotype that once upon a time London was populated largely by a haughty collection of politicians, royalty and hangers-on. But mix in the joyful playfulness of the the city's new architectural wonders – the giant observation wheel, the London Eye, is possibly the winning example – and you've got the London of today, where traditionalism and modernism co-exist in a unique blend which gives the city a tangible character that can't be matched in other cities.

Bigger in area than most cities, London is divided into two by its most distinct feature, the River Thames. The debate over whether south London or north London is the better part of the city rages on. Greater London is made up of the City of London and 32 boroughs, each run by individual councils. The different parts of the city are grouped together and categorised simply as north, south, east, west and central.

Nearly eight million people live in the city itself, with another 12 million in the wider metropolitan area. Over 10% of the UK's population live here, and it is also home to millions of 'temporary' residents who pass through each year. London's demography is a colourful one: almost one third of Londoners are from an ethnic background, so you can expect to hear many different languages, experience many different cultures, and sample the cuisines of many different countries.

Culture

Vibrant and alive with a heady cultural mix, London is the world's most diverse city. From its cockney rhyming slang to its fabulous festivals, and from great fish and chips to formal afternooon tea, there's something for every taste.

A City of Colours

Few cities can boast a more vibrant mix of people and cultures than London. It is one of the most diverse capitals in the world, and perhaps because of this it is hard to talk about one overall, dominant cultural way of life. From the huge Bangladeshi population in east London to the Portuguese stronghold of Stockwell, London's ethnic communities are large and varied. Indeed, one of the city's major festivals, the Notting Hill Carnival, celebrates Afro-Caribbean culture. Sizeable pockets of temporary migrants, such as Australians, South Africans and eastern Europeans, also form significant communities across the capital.

It's not just foreigners who are drawn to London however; larger numbers of the city's population are from elsewhere in the UK, usually for professional reasons.

It would be incorrect to say London is a totally harmonious place – race-related tensions do occur, and immigration is a sensitive subject in UK politics. But on the whole, Londoners are proud of their city's diversity and the fact that it remains one of the most tolerant and welcoming cities in Europe.

Food & Drink

London's culinary reputation has taken a turn for the better in recent years – far from being the capital of bland and stodgy fare, the city is home to some of the most diverse and high-quality eateries in Europe (and is one of the top four cities in the world to eat out in, according to the *Zagat Survey 2005*). From African and Afghan to Polish and Peruvian, the range of cuisine reflects the multicultural composition of the city. There has also been a much-heralded revival in British food and local produce.

Perhaps the quintessential English culinary tradition is the famous Sunday roast, but British cuisine ranges from the old favourite of fish and chips (still sold wrapped in newspaper) to the delicacies of afternoon tea in upmarket hotels like the Ritz.

Chinese food is consistently popular (head for Chinatown for the best), and you won't struggle to find a great Indian curry – Brick Lane in the East End and Southall to the west have some of the best curry houses in the UK.

The Sunday Roast

You can't leave the UK without tucking into a succulent Sunday roast, a tradition dating back to World War II. Expect a roasted joint of meat (beef, lamb, pork or chicken), accompanied by roast potatoes, assorted vegetables, gravy and often Yorkshire pudding (a baked batter of flour, milk and eggs). It's a firm Sunday fixture on most pub menus, where it's normally washed down with a pint of beer – leading to another one of Britain's great Sunday traditions – the afternoon nap.

Drinking is a significant factor in the culture of London, and one that has few restrictions (apart from how much your body can take). It may not have its own wine regions, but ask any Brit about the qualities of a good pint, and you've got a connoisseur's conversation in the making.

Economy, Employment & Industry

London has Europe's largest economy and, along with New York and Tokyo, is a major global powerhouse. Domestically, it accounts for around one-fifth of the country's GDP. On the international stage, London has many advantages that give it the edge over other economic centres, including Britain's friendly relationship with the US, the widespread use of the English language and law throughout the business world, and the capital's position as a major aviation hub. London's multi-culturalism – one of its main selling points – is another attraction for international business.

The British economy is currently bouyant, and growing by around 2% each year. London plays a major role in this success – the city has a huge workforce (around 3.4 million) and salaries are about 20% higher than elsewhere in the country. The downside is the high cost of living – rents are astronomical and 750,000 people commute to work from outside the capital every day.

Finance is London's largest industry. Canary Wharf now acts as a second financial centre, and includes the worldwide headquarters of many influential finance companies. While it is not larger than the finance industry, the city's creative industry is one of the most significant. It is a highly competitive area and jobs in advertising, design, fashion, film, music, publishing, radio and TV are coveted by many.

Language

English is London's primary language, although approximately 300 others are spoken in the city. It's not out of the ordinary to hear people ordering breakfast in Italian, chatting in Urdu on the tube, or talking on their mobile in Turkish. Nearly all instructions and signs are written in English.

Cockney rhyming slang is famous for its humorous slant on the language. It works by replacing words with short, rhyming phrases, so 'boat race' means face, and 'apples and pears' means stairs. But sometimes abbreviations remove the rhyme and make it harder to understand: 'plates' means feet (from 'plates of meat') and 'bees' means money (from 'bees and honey'). It's hard to understand, but that's the whole point!

London slang is today veering away from the traditional as the recent influx of other cultures, like Bengali, exert their influence.

Religion

The mix of faiths in London is as diverse as the language, with all major world religions represented. Historically the city has been dominated by Christianity and there are a large number of churches in the capital. A large majority of English people are nominally Christian, although those that attend regular church services are in a minority. Anglicanism is the main denomination of Christianity in the UK, and is led by the Archbishop of Canterbury, whose main residence is Lambeth Place.

History

History and London go hand in hand – the city has seen wars and bloodshed, plagues and rebellions – and millions of visitors from around the world visit the capital to get a slice of the tradition for which the city is renowned.

Despite the periodical destruction of large chunks of London across the ages, through fire and attack, there is still plenty of history to see, from palaces and parliament to cathedrals and cobbled streets. London's story stretches back 2,000 years to Roman times, when invaders expanding their empire westwards settled on the banks of the Thames. Over the next three centuries, the settlement grew to become Londinium, until it was abandoned in the fifth century, and fragments of the town's wall are still visible today amid the modern offices in London's financial district.

The Missing Millennium

The legacy of life over the next thousand years is pretty scarce. After the Romans, London was an area of settlement, invasion and resettlement, hosting Saxons, Vikings and Normans under varying degrees of violence. The city was then burnt to the ground. The trend of building things out of wood, and too close together, meant that large sections of the city were periodically destroyed by fire. One of the more notable remnants from this period is Westminster Abbey, built by

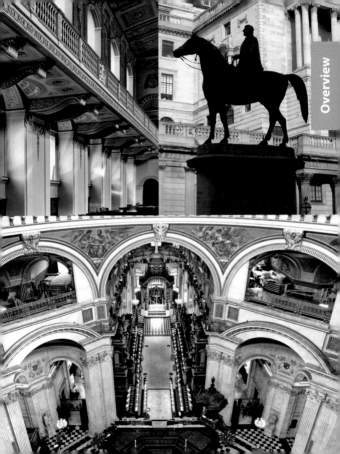

Edward the Confessor, the last Anglo-Saxon king of England. Less than a year after it was built, Norman conquerer William was coronated there, beginning a new chaper of English history and starting the royal lineage that, to some degree, continues today. Although the abbey has been rebuilt, you can still see parts of the original in the arches and columns of the cloisters. William was also responsible for ordering the construction of part of the Tower of London.

In 1666, the overcrowded, dirty and disease-ridden city of London was effectively wiped out by the Great Fire, which burned for five days. Architect Sir Christopher Wren was the major figure in the post-fire reconstruction, designing many of the churches dotted around the city, including the iconic St Paul's Cathedral.

Industrialisation

Development gathered pace during the 18th and 19th centuries, with the population increasing and polarising rapidly. The industrial revolution made the rich wealthier and empirical expansion transformed Britain into the major world superpower of the age. The 'haves' lived in plush residential squares and large terraced townhouses, while the 'have-nots' struggled to get by in slum areas of the city. Crime rates soared, eventually leading to the formation of the early police force, the Bow Street Runners.

A significant contribution of the times was the development of public transport. The first subterranean train route was opened in 1863, and the first electric track was in place less than 30 years later.

Twentieth Century

The start of the 20th century saw entertainment and glamour taking a foothold in the city, in contrast to the straight-laced attitudes of the Victorian era. New cafes, theatres and hotels, including the Ritz, played host to a lively social scene.

London was hugely affected by the first world war, not just because of the 600 or so that died in air raids – poor post-war conditions resulted in housing and labour difficulties, which in turn brought strikes and civil disturbances.

Things got worse in the early 30s, thanks to an economic depression. As the decade progressed, the city grew both in population and in area.

The second world war was perhaps the city's darkest hour: bombing during the Blitz of 1940 and 1941 destroyed large parts of London and killed thousands.

Post-War Years

The austere post-war years were lit up by the staging of the Olympics at Wembley in 1948 and the Festival of Britain in 1951. As Britain returned to prosperity, labour shortages led to a policy of attracting immigrants to the capital to share the workload. This was the beginning of London's multicultural transformation,

Killer Fog

In 1952, a smog engulfed London for four days, bringing the capital to a standstill. Caused by the combination of excessive coal burning and freezing temperatures, the air quality was so poor that it is estimated to have caused the death of about 4,000 people. The crisis led to the imposition of laws to phase out 'dirty fuels' and black smoke.

as different ethnic groups settled into different areas and formed strong, growing communities.

In the 60s London was where legends were made: the hip areas of Carnaby Street and King's Road, an exploding film and music scene, the World Cup victory and a vivacious party scene marked the beginning of London's reputation as a cutting edge capital for arts and fashion. The party didn't last into the 70s though, as harsh economic conditions led to civil unrest and IRA bombing campaigns started in the city. Margaret Thatcher's right-wing stronghold in the 80s did little to ease the mood, and her government's policies resulted in high unemployment and a widening gap between the rich and the poor.

After Tony Blair came to power in 1997, London enjoyed a new-found reputation as a hip city when news of 'cool Britannia' spread around the globe.

A New Era

Today London enjoys a healthy economic climate that has seen housing prices soar and unemployment rates drop. The city successfully bid to host the 2012 Olympics, which is expected to provide jobs, investment, and further regeneration. The day after London was awarded the games, a terrorist attack on three tube trains and a bus killed 52 people. While the attacks had a sobering impact on the lives of all residents, resilient Londoners were determined to carry on with 'business as usual'. As on many occasions over the last 2,000 years, London has picked itself up, and the story of this remarkable city is set to keep on unfolding.

London timeline

43	Romans settle in the Thames Valley
1055	Westminster Abbey is completed
1078	Work starts on The Tower of London
1170	Population of London exceeds 30,000
1176	Construction begins on London Bridge
1591	First Shakespeare play at the Globe Theatre
1605	Guy Fawkes and collaborators attempt, and fail, to assasinate King James I
1665	The Great Plague; 60,000 Londoners die
1666	Great Fire of London destroys half of the city
1707	The Act of Union is passed, merging Scotland and England
1708	St Paul's Cathedral is completed
1750	The Bow Street Runners (early police force) are formed
1750	Westminster Bridge opens
1829	The Metropolitan Police force is formed
1845	Construction of Trafalgar Square completed
1849	Harrods is opened (as a grocery store) by Charles Henry Harrod
1858	Construction of Big Ben is completed
1863	Construction begins on the London Underground
1877	The first public electric lighting in London

1908	Olympic games is held in London
1914	First World War begins
1918	First World War ends
1923	Wembley Stadium opens
1939	Second World War begins
1940	Winston Churchill becomes prime minister
1945	Second World War ends
1948	The Olympics Games held at Wembley Stadium
1952	The Great Smog hits London
1953	Coronation of Queen Elizabeth II
1959	The first Notting Hill Carnival takes place
1965	The Greater London Council (GLC) formed
1966	England hosts and wins the World Cup
1979	Margaret Thatcher becomes prime minister
1985	Live Aid takes place in Wembley, attended by more than 70,000 people
1997	Tony Blair becomes prime minister
1997	Diana Spencer dies in a Paris car crash; mourners pour into London for the funeral
1999	The London Eye is opened by Tony Blair
2005	Live 8 takes place in Hyde Park
2005	London wins the 2012 Olympics bid
2005	Terrorist bombings kill 52 commuters and injure hundreds of Londoners

London Today

London's rich heritage and iconic landmarks have been attracting visitors for years. Today, with the focus on improved facilities, the city is widening its appeal.

London stands proud as one of the world's greatest destinations, attracting thousands of visitors every year. Thanks to relaxed attitudes to diversity and its position as a major European and global economic powerhouse, the city can look forward to continued development and prosperity in the future.

Various new developments have been planned in recent years, particularly within the transport and leisure industries. The rebuilding of Wembley Stadium, England's national football arena, has been one of the major projects in the capital over the last decade, although it has not been without its controversies. Completion is long past schedule and way over budget, although on the plus side the scheme has included significant upgrading of transport infrastructure in north-west London.

Government & Politics

Britain is a constitutional monarchy, whereby the monarch acts as head of state while an elected parliament makes and passes legislation. The current monarch is Queen Elizabeth II, who has held the throne since 1952. The heir to the throne is

Charles, Prince of Wales. Although the Queen would appear to be a powerful figure, it can be argued that she has little effect on law or policy making – these roles are led more by parliament and the prime minister.

At time of going to print, Tony Blair was the prime minister of Britain, although he is expected to step down during the course of 2007 and hand the title to Gordon Brown.

The City of London has its own administration, which is coordinated by the Greater London Authority (GLA). The principal figure of the GLA is the mayor of London, who is democratically elected every four years and has executive powers covering London's planning, transport, policing, economic development and cultural activities. Ken Livingstone has been the mayor of London since 2000, and was re-elected for another term in 2004. Undoubtedly his most high-profile move to date has been to introduce the Congestion Charge to reduce traffic congestion in central London, a move welcomed by some but equally heavily criticised by others.

Livingstone can be credited with keeping a focus on various environmental issues, and with creating the London Climate Change Agency. His liberal attitude to same-sex partnerships can also be commended: although the current London Partnership Register is still one step shy of recognising full marriage, the partners in a same-sex relationship are recognised and awarded almost all the same rights as married couples.

The mayor was wholeheartedly praised, however, for his backing of London's bid to host the 2012 Olympic Games.

The bid was successful, and is expected to create thousands of jobs across a range of sectors including transport, construction, service and hospitality, and media. Related investment and development will inject new life into deprived parts of east London as new facilities and infrastructure are built. Transport developments form a major part of planning for the games, with station renovations and line extensions on the drawing board.

Tourism

According to Visit London, approximately 24.5 million visitors flocked to the city in 2005 to take in the heritage, iconic landmarks and cultural attractions, and spent around £9 billion in the process. The tourism industry is bouyant, and supports an estimated 350,000 jobs directly or indirectly.

The industy has been hit by various political and natural hurdles, however. The 9/11 attacks in New York sent ripples of fear around the world, adversely affecting the tourism industry in general. The London bombings of 2005, the domestic outbreaks of foot and mouth disease, the international outbreak of SARS and the weakening of the dollar against the pound have done little to aid industry recovery. However, while visitor numbers have not returned to the levels of 2000, both domestic and international tourism remain strong, supported by the rising number of cheap European flights in the last few years.

Recent additions to London's list of attractions, including the London Eye (p.56) and the Tate Modern (p.103), have proved popular. Pre-Olympics investment, the opening of a fifth terminal at Heathrow, among other developments, should help to increase the number of international visitors.

Environmental Issues

London bears the pressure of millions of visitors and residents creating waste, consuming electricity and driving cars, all of which have a massive negative impact on the environment. However, the mayor's focus on green issues, as well as the need to fall in line with EU regulations, mean that environmental considerations are a priority for the city. Currently, around 11% of household waste is recycled, although this is expected to rise to 25% by 2008.

London's River Thames was declared 'biologically dead' as little as 50 years ago, due to the level of water pollution. However, environmental controls have vastly improved the situation and the river is home to abundant marine life.

Poor air quality is estimated to cause 1,600 premature deaths in the city each year, although the introduction of a Low Emission Zone, which will ban polluting vehicles from the roads, is expected to improve matters. The mayor's energy strategy will see London switch production from fossil fuels to renewable sources over the next decade.

Stop the Pigeons

Gone are the days when tourists could feed the pigeons in Trafalgar Square – the mayor banned feeding them and ordered a cull, which has reduced the number of pigeons in the square to just a few hundred. Animal rights activists continue to feed the birds in the northern part of the square.

Exploring

London Pride

London is a city of a thousand icons. From Camden's punks to Traitor's Gate, its history and culture are always visible and mix with a modern vibrancy that can be felt on every street. Time to explore...

London is the home of Big Ben and Piccadilly Circus, the royal family and those familiar red double-decker buses, but its heritage stretches back over hundreds of years. Pre-Roman settlements have been discovered along the Thames, and the city was established following Roman invasion in AD43. The heart of Londinium was the area we now know as the City – the capital's financial quarter – and traces of the Roman era can still be seen today amid the skyscrapers.

Londoners tend to think of their city as a series of villages, and its many neighbourhoods within the capital's 32 boroughs possess a character that is distinctly their own, be it the reggae-infused street culture of Brixton, the elegantly refined charms of leafy Hampstead or the gritty urbanity of central London itself. Visitors tend to begin in the centre, where the energy of Soho and Chinatown, the world-famous Theatreland and the almost tangible history of the newly regenerated East End evoke the rich vibrancy and variety of the capital's ancient and recent past.

What really captures visitors' imaginations, however, is the powerful iconography of the city, from the pomp of Buckingham Palace to the ceremony of the Houses of Parliament. Mix in the sheer joyful playfulness of the architectural wonders of the new skyline, like the London Eye or the 'Gherkin', and you have that heady mix of traditional and modern that London does so well.

London's heritage, history and reputation, as both a top party destination and the gateway to the rest of western Europe, continues to draw tourists from every corner of the globe. And when they get here, their preconceptions are confounded again by a city that isn't just tall buildings and ancient monuments, but filled with more beautiful and accessible green spaces than any other city of its size.

Londoners are justifiably proud of the city they live in. They may have a practical cynicism about aspects of the city's infrastructure, but retain a real pride in its many positives. They have good reason; the heritage and history visible in so many streets, the cosmopolitan cultural mix that sees 300 different languages spoken every day, the world-class shopping, arts and entertainment and the cultural treasures and museums all combine to make this a place that always fascinates and surprises.

Beyond the M25

London is the transport hub for the UK. From here, you can get a sleeper train to the far north of Scotland, head off to the Lake District in Cumbria or go west and explore the Cotswolds or on into Wales. London's four airports and Luton also mean that air travellers are well served, with a host of budget airlines battling to take you on super-cheap European excursions. See p.190 of the Visitors' Info chapter for more.

London Essentials

Take a Double-Decker Bus

London's iconic buses are a great way to get the lie of the land and are far cheaper than black cabs. Or you can try one of the hop-on, hop-off bus tour companies based around Marble Arch and Baker Street.

Cruise the Thames

A river cruise along the Thames by day or night is a spectacular way to see the city's great landmarks, from the Houses of Parliament to 30 St Mary Axe (known locally as the 'Gherkin') just along from Tower Bridge.

Dance in the Streets

Every August bank holiday, the streets of west London come alive to the Caribbean rhythms of the Notting Hill Carnival. Europe's biggest street party takes place over two days, regularly drawing up to one million revellers.

Explore the City's Canals

If the Thames is at the heart of London, then its many canals and waterways are its arteries. While no longer integral to transport and commerce, these canals make picturesque places for a stroll or a picnic.

Enjoy a Curry

You will find Indian curry houses on every high street in London, but for a particularly memorable meal try visiting the so-called 'curry corridor' on Tooting High Street and nearby Upper Tooting Road, or in Brick Lane.

Go to a Gig

Whatever style of music you prefer, there will be a live performance to cater to your tastes somewhere in London on any night of the week. Wembley Arena, Brixton Academy, Ronnie Scott's and Camden's grungy Barfly are just some of the top venues.

Visit a Street Market

Camden for furniture and goth-hippy chic, Portobello for antiques and fashion and Borough for every foodie's dream – London's street markets are some of the best in the world. Find a good one and you'll never want to visit a supermarket again.

Lose Yourself in a Museum

The number of galleries and museums in town is too numerous to name. Suffice to say that whether your interests lie in archaeological treasures, the history of art and design or just great art, London has all of the above and more.

Stroll the South Bank

Walk up-river from Tower Hill, taking in the 'Gherkin', Shakespeare's Globe and Tate Modern, then stroll past the street performers and skateboarders. Enjoy a drink at the open-air National Film Theatre bar, before finishing your journey at the foot of the London Eye.

Have a Pint with the Locals

Whether it's a preserved old Victorian boozer converted into a fashionable gastropub or a spit-and-sawdust number where the same old geezers have been propping up the bar for years, London is home to no end of decent pubs. Cheers!

Take a 'Flight' on the London Eye

Housing 32 giant, sealed walk-on pods, the Eye offers breathtaking views for up to 25 miles in all directions across the city. Try it just as night falls and watch as London's concrete jungle is replaced by shimmering lights.

Discover a Secret Garden

London has many little patches of green tucked away in the heart of the city that provide a great way to escape. Whether you choose the bustling vibe of Soho Square or the surprising quiet of Russell Square, you're in for a peaceful (re)treat.

West End

From the neon lights of Piccadilly Circus to the brashness of Soho and star-studded Theatreland, London's West End is an attraction in itself.

The West End attracts tourists and natives in search of the best of London's culture and entertainment. Here you'll find Soho's buzzing alleyways, a genuine Chinatown, Covent Garden's packed piazza and the entertainment hubs of Piccadilly Circus and Leicester Square. And there's more theatres than you can shake a thesp at.
*For **restaurants and bars**, see p.150, p.156 and p.160.*

Chinatown
Between Shaftesbury Avenue and Leicester Square lies London's Chinatown. Don't let the gimmicky pagodas fool you into thinking that this area is anything but authentic – Chinese families settled in the area in the 1950s, opening the first of the many restaurants for which the district is now famous, and the surrounding streets are at the heart of the capital's Chinese New Year celebrations. If you're heading to a show in one of the many theatres on Shaftesbury Avenue, Chinatown is the perfect place to pop for a bite to eat before or after the evening's entertainment. You can also get a pedicab – a kind of cycle rickshaw – from here back to your hotel at the end of the night (as long as you're not staying too far out of town).

Map A **1**

West End

Royal Opera House
London Transport Museum
Covent Garden Market
Zimbabwe House
Strand
Bow St
Floral St
Russell St
Southampton St
Adam St
John Adam St
Durham St
Covent Garden
Bedford St
Endell St
Langley St
Mercer St
New Row
Police Station
William IV St
St Martin's Lane
COVENT GARDEN 2
Oasis Sports Centre
Betterton St
Neal St
St Giles High St
Earlham St
Monmouth St
St Martin's Ln
St Martins Theatre
Shaftesbury Ave
Stacey St
Charing Cross Rd
Leicester Sq
St Martin's Pl
Newport Pl
Lisle St
CHINATOWN 1
National Gallery
Cranbourn St
Whitcomb St
Coventry St
Centrepoint
Charing Cross Rd
Denmark St
Flitcroft St
Palace Theatre
Prince Edward Theatre
Hazlitt's
Soho St
Sutton Row
Old Compton St
Moor St
Romilly St
Greek St
Frith St
Dean St
Wardour St
Windmill St
Gt Windmill St
Rupert St
Trocadero Centre
Criterion Theatre
Piccadilly Circus
Haymarket
Regent St
St Alban's St
Air St
Glasshouse St
Brewer St
Denman St
Sherwood St
Richmond Mews
Oxford St
Soho Sq
Carlisle St
Bateman St
Meard St
Broadwick St
Berwick St
Hopkins St
Ingestre Pl
Lexington St
Gt Pulteney St
Bridle Lane
Beak St
Warwick St
Glasshouse St
Dean St
Gr. Chapel St
Wardour St
Gt Marlborough St
Duck La
Bourchier St
Tyler's Ct
Peter St
Nigel Playfair Av
Poland St
Marshall St
SOHO 4
3

500m N

Covent Garden

Covent Garden attracts so many visitors that it can be unbearably crowded at times, but look beyond the bustling piazza, with its weird and wonderful – and sometimes downright awful – street performers, and the attractive but uninspired covered market, and there is much to charm the visitor. A highlight is Neal's Yard, with its famous cheese shop, wholefood sellers and slightly hippyish feel, while Seven Dials is sleek and chic, home to a lovely selection of boutiques and cafes. London's Transport Museum (7565 7299) offers an interesting insight into the history of the tube and bus network, and is a particular winner with children (it's scheduled to reopen in November 2007 after refurbishment). In the piazza itself, the Royal Opera House (7304 4000) offers tours of its splendid, revamped building; the backstage visits are a treat.

Map A **2**

Piccadilly Circus & Leicester Square

The neon brashness of Piccadilly Circus is one of the capital's most famous landmarks, and it's always heaving with traffic and tourists milling around the legendary Statue of Eros. A little further along Piccadilly, the food hall at historic department store Fortnum & Mason (see p.136) never fails to delight, but if it's views you're after head to Waterstone's. The 5th View bar and cafe (7851 2433) on the top floor of Europe's largest bookshop offers a sweeping vista across London and is a perfect place to unwind after pounding the galleries of the nearby Royal Academy of Arts. The golden art deco interior of the Criterion restaurant (0871 2238045) is stunning, and is perfect for a pre-theatre cocktail or two. Between Piccadilly Circus and Leicester Square is the London Trocadero (09068 881100), which is home to an amusement arcade, bowling alley, cinema and a few bars. The main attraction in Leicester Square itself is the Odeon, the venue for star-studded, red carpet film premieres and awards ceremonies. There are also a few hand prints of famous actors, and you can pick up half-price tickets to a selection of West End shows from the square's 'tkts' booth.

Map A **3**

Soho

It may have always had a reputation for seediness, but Soho has cleaned up its act a fair bit in recent times. Once most famous for its strip bars and sex shops, Soho is now known as the centre of the capital's film industry (around Wardour Street), the heart of its gay community (focused on Old Compton Street) and for its reputation as being home to a particularly louche arts and literary scene. Roughly demarcated by Oxford Street, Charing Cross Road, Shaftesbury Avenue and Regent Street, this is one of the most bustling parts of the city. And it's not all pubs and nightlife either – Berwick Street offers the twin delights of the city centre's only authentic fruit and veg market and some of the best fabric shops in town, while an afternoon spent people-watching in Soho Square is a must. Look out for the park bench that commemorates the late singer Kirsty MacColl.

Map A **4**

If you only do one thing in...
West End

Get yourself a half-priced ticket from Leicester Square for a show on Shaftesbury Avenue, the heart of Theatreland.

Best for...

Eating: Take your pick from the scores of authentic Cantonese restaurants in Chinatown.

Drinking: Order a pint in one of Soho's heaving old boozers and watch the area's colourful characters come and go (p.150).

Sightseeing: It may be dirty, overcrowded and choked with traffic, but a photo of the neon lights of Piccadilly Circus should be on every visitor's checklist (p.36).

Shopping: Whether you prefer the department stores on Oxford Street or the chic outlets of Covent Garden, the West End is a shopper's paradise.

Outdoor: Spend a sunny afternoon relaxing in the garden of Soho Square and let the whole of central London rush by (p.37).

Westminster & Strand

This is the heart of London's establishment. Home to the Queen and the Houses of Parliament, the area positively reeks of history and power, from medieval times to the modern day.

Here you'll find the world's most famous front door, a clock with a bell known around the world and the official residence of the Queen of England. But even away from the popular tours, you can see the history on every street.
*For **restaurants and bars** in the area, see p.160.*

Buckingham Palace

The Mall, SW1

7766 7300
www.royal.gov.uk

The Queen's official residence in London is an imposing 775 room building at the south-west end of the Mall. The royal residence opens for a few months over the summer while the Queen is away; the throne room, state dining room and music room – where Prince Charles and Prince William were christened – are among the 19 rooms and gardens that are opened to the public. The Queen's Gallery was reopened in 2002 to show off part of the Royal Collection – an astonishing anthology of treasures, featuring works by Leonardo da Vinci, Rubens and Canaletto. Also on display are lavish furnishings, jewellery, sculptures, ceramics, and works by Faberge.

⊖ St James's Park

Map B 1

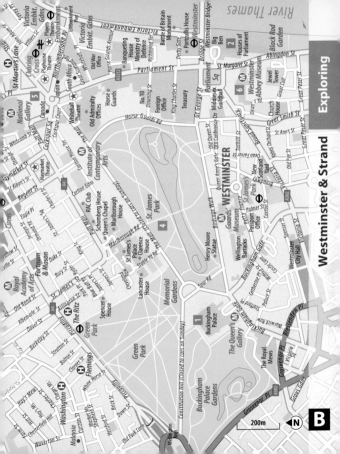

River Thames

St-Martin's Lane
Victoria Embkt. Gdns
Player's Theatre
Embankment Pier
Victoria Embkt. Gdns
Battle of Britain Monument
Portcullis House
Westminster Bridge
Big Ben **2**
Houses of Parliament
Black Rod Garden
Abingdon St.

St Martin's Pl.
Charing Cross
Playhouse Theatre
South Africa
Old War Office
Banqueting House
Ministry of Defence
Richmond Ter.
Derby Gate
Bridge St.
St Margaret St.
Westminster Abbey Museum **6**
Jewel Tower
Great Coll.
Great Peter St.

National Gallery
Whitcomb St.
Cockspur Court
Canada
Japan
Whitehall
South Africa
Old Admiralty Offices
Horse Guards
Parliament St.
No.10 Downing St.
Foreign Office
King Charles St.
Treasury
Gt George St.
St George St.
Middlesex Guildhall
Church House
Great Smith St.
St Ann's Gt.
Great Peter St.

Haymarket St.
St Alban's St.
Regent St.
Haymarket
Theatre
New Zealand
Carlton House Ter.
Institute of Contemporary Arts
Horse Guards Rd.
WESTMINSTER
Queen Anne's Gate
QEII Conference Ctr
Old Queen St.
Dean Farrar St.
New Scotland Yard
St Ann's St.
Noel's Orchard St.
Old Pye St.

Circus
Eagle Pl.
Jermyn St.
St James's St.
Duke St.
RAC Club
Schomberg House
Queen's Chapel
Marlborough House
St. James's Park
Guards' Museum
St James's Park
Birdcage Walk
Palmer St.
Caxton St.
Passport Office
New St.
Broadway

Fortnum & Mason
Royal Academy of Arts
Old Bond St.
Albemarle St.
Dover St.
St. James's St.
Bury St.
King St.
St James's Sq.
Marlborough Rd.
St James's Palace
Clarence House
Stable Yd Rd.
Lancaster House
Henry Moore Statue
Wellington Barracks
Buckingham Gate
Victoria St.
Westminster City Hall
Caxton Pl.
Stafford Pl.
Warwick Row

Swallow St.
Piccadilly
The Ritz
Green Park
Spencer House
Memorial Gardens
Spur Rd.
Buckingham Palace **1**
The Queen's Gallery
The Royal Mews
Buckingham Gate
Buckingham Palace Rd.
Warwick Row
Bressenden Pl.

Berkeley St.
Stratton St.
Bolton St.
Half Moon St.
White Horse St.
Flemings
Green Park
Green Park
Buckingham Palace Gardens
Grosvenor Pl.
Grosvenor Gdns.
Lower Grosvenor Pl.

Hay's Mews
Charles St.
Chesterfield Hill
Waverton St.
Market Mews
Shepherd St.
Washington
Malaysia
Brick St.
Down St.
Constitution Hill (closed to cars on Sunday)
Old Park Lane
Wellington Arch

200m

N **B**

Houses of Parliament

Parliament Square, SW1

7219 3000
www.parliament.uk

To many, the giant clock tower commonly known as Big Ben isn't just a geographical landmark, but the very symbol of London itself. It might come as a surprise, then, to know that the tower ('Big Ben' is actually the name of the bell inside) has been a feature of the skyline for less than 150 years.

In 1834 a fire destroyed most of the Houses of Parliament, leading to the construction of much of the building that stands today. Charles Barry's bold Gothic structure bore the brunt of a bombing raid during the Blitz in 1941, destroying the House of Commons chamber. Architect Sir Giles Gilbert Scott designed its five-story replacement, which opened in 1950; the imposing structure has remained largely unchanged since then. Much of the building can be visited – the Jewel Tower and chapel crypt are open year-round

– while one-hour tours of the clock tower can be arranged in advance by contacting Members of Parliament.

⊖ Westminster

Map B **2**

Somerset House

The Strand, WC2

7845 4600
www.somerset-house.org.uk

Situated on the Strand, one of central London's main arteries, lies the imposing and beautifully restored 18th century Somerset House, the city's first purpose-built office block. The site is now home to the shiny decorative treasures of the Gilbert Collection and the Hermitage Rooms – the display of which recreates in miniature the Winter Palace in St Petersburg, from which the collection is on long-term loan. Best of all, however, is the jewel-like Courtauld Institute Gallery. Occupying the northern wing of the building is this staggering collection, which includes works by Dutch master Rubens, and Manet's post-impressionist masterpiece, *Bar at the Folies-Bergere*. Other attractions lie away from the house's collections. The Great Courtyard is home to impressive display fountains in the summer and a much-loved winter ice-skating rink, while the terrace offers splendid views over the Thames.

⊖ Temple

Map B **3**

St James's Park & Green Park

SW1

7930 1793
www.royalparks.gov.uk

St James's Park's royal associations and location at the heart of some of London's major attractions makes it one of the most visited parks in Europe (around 5.5 million people pass through each year), but it still manages to retain an air of tranquil calm. One of its top draws is the small colony of pelicans that live near Duck Island. The birds were first introduced in 1664 and their daily feed at 15:00 is a much-loved ritual that's frequently enlivened by their brazen mingling with the park's human visitors. Considerably quieter, nearby Green Park's 40 acres of grassland is the link between St James's Park and Hyde Park. While lacking both the pomp and ceremony of its renowned neighbours, the park is not without its historical significance (it was a duelling ground until 1887), and its mature trees and grassland make the park a favourite spot for Londoners to escape the bustle of the city.

⊖ St. James's Park/Green Park

Map B **4**

Trafalgar Square

WC1   www.london.gov.uk/trafalgarsquare

Just south of the West End is the revamped Trafalgar Square, the 'crossroads of London' and home to the towering Nelson's column (and former home of thousands of pigeons). It's surrounded by impressive buildings and galleries, including the National Gallery (7747 2885) and National Portrait Gallery, and the fascinating St Martin-in-the-Fields church, complete with excellent cafe (7766 1100). Trafalgar Square has long been a focal point for Londoners; it's a magnet for rallies, protests and celebrations and was traditionally the place where hardy locals swam in the fountains to welcome in the new year (something that's not encouraged now). Renovation work to improve the square, including pedestrianising the northern side, cleaning up the fountain and, controversially, getting rid of the pigeons, was completed in 2003. ⇌ ⊖ Charing Cross

Map B **5**

Westminster Abbey

7654 4900

Parliament Square, SW1   www.westminster-abbey.org

A must-see for anyone on London's heritage trail, Westminster Abbey is known as the House of Kings – the place where English royalty is both crowned and buried (every monarch since William the Conqueror has been coronated in the abbey). Poets' Corner is particularly notable as the resting place for some of England's greatest literary figures, including Geoffrey Chaucer, writer of *The Canterbury Tales*, and TS Eliot. Others, including Shakespeare, have had commemorative plaques erected here in their honour. Elsewhere, the grave of the Unknown Warrior, close to the West Door, has long been a site of pilgrimage. For all its history, the abbey is very much a functioning place of worship. Services are held every day and a comprehensive line-up of concerts and lectures runs throughout the year and all are welcome. If you have the chance attend a service to get the full measure of the church in all its glory, and revel in wonder as the notes of the choristers soar into the furthest reaches of one of the world's great ecclesiastical monuments.

⊖ Westminster

Map B **6**

If you only do one thing in...
Westminster & Strand

Get up close (and almost personal) with British royalty on a tour round Buckingham Palace, home of the Queen.

Best for...

Eating: Dine in style at the Strand's Savoy Grill (p.160) – the chef's cooked for the Queen, you know.

Drinking: Order a cocktail from the rooftop bar of The Trafalgar hotel on the south side of the square for superb views across central London.

Sightseeing: Take a stroll around Parliament Square and marvel at two British institutions – the Houses of Parliament (p.42) and Westminster Abbey (p.45).

Shopping: Forget the high-class boutiques and famous department stores – buy yourself a tacky memento from one of the area's many souvenir stalls.

Outdoor: It's not often you get to feed the pelicans in the UK – but head to St James's Park at 15:00 and you can do just that (see p.43).

The City

Swarming with suits on weekdays, deserted on weekends, the City is the financial centre of London – some would say the world – but there's more to the area than banking and trading.

There is something inspiring about the austerity of London's golden mile. Once the pinstripes are gone, the area is an architectural momument to Britain's trading past and present, which can be appreciated in almost complete silence. And nearby is the glory of St Pauls and the gruesome history of the Tower. *For restaurants and bars in the area, see p.162.*

Barbican Centre

Silk Street, EC2

7638 8891
www.barbican.org.uk

As stark a piece of 1960s architecture as the Southbank Centre across the river, the Barbican Centre too has been equally lauded and reviled by critics. Developed as part of a rebuilding project after the area was severely damaged by bombing raids during the second world war, it contains a big residential development as well as a splendid arts centre, complete with galleries, theatres and an excellent cinema. There's also history on display here too – a bastion of the original Roman wall can be seen above ground in the churchyard of St Giles' Cripplegate, located in the heart of the centre, while nearby Smithfield Market has been around for over 800 years and is still going strong. Today it employs over

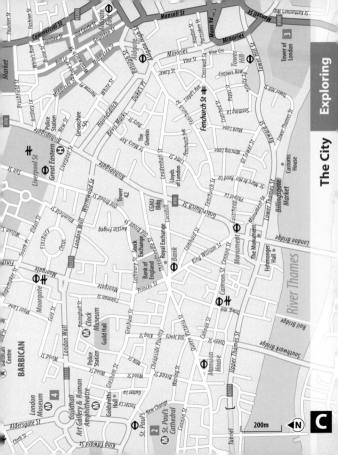

BARBICAN

River Thames

London Bridge

Southwark Bridge

Tower of London

St. Paul's Cathedral

Bank of England

Royal Exchange

Stock Exchange

The Monument

Mansion House

Guild Hall

Clock Museum

London Museum

Goldsmiths Hall

Customs House

Billingsgate Market

Fishmonger Hall

Lloyds of London

The Gherkin

Tower 42

Great Eastern

Police Station

Liverpool St

Fenchurch St

Aldgate

Aldgate East

Moorgate

Monument

200m

N

C

3,000 people, has its own meat market and is one of the few places with early-opening pubs (an old licensing law states that a pub next to a market can open as early as 05:30).

⊖ Barbican

Map C **1**

St Paul's Cathedral
Ludgate Hill, EC4

7236 4128
www.stpauls.co.uk

Designed by Sir Christopher Wren as part of a massive rebuilding project after the Great Fire in 1666, the famous cathedral is the fifth church dedicated to St Paul to stand on the site. It was built between 1675 and 1710 (the first service took place in 1697), and the architecture is stunning. The Whispering Gallery in the dome is worth a visit even if its magical acoustics are often drowned out by the sheer volume of people trying to put them to the test. Downstairs, the crypt is fascinating, while the main organ, installed in 1695, was once played by the composer Mendelssohn. St Paul's has been the focus of much of the capital's spiritual life, from the funerals of Lord Nelson and Winston Churchill to the marriage of Charles and Diana and, more recently, memorial services for those killed in the 2005 tube bombings. A service is held here every day.

⊖ St Paul's

Map C **2**

Tower Bridge & Tower of London
Tower Hill, EC1

7403 3761
www.towerbridge.org.uk

For a long time neighbouring London Bridge was the only connection between the north and south banks of the Thames.

When it opened in 1894, Tower Bridge was considered to be one of the great feats of modern industrial engineering, the largest and most complex bascule (counterbalanced) bridge ever built. Hydraulic power still opens the bascules, even if, since 1976, oil and electricity rather than the original steam has driven them. A comprehensive account of the bridge's history can be seen in the exhibition in the high-level walkways, which had been closed to the public since 1910 following a lack of use (people preferred to wait and watch the bascules rise rather than access the walkways themselves). On the northern side of the bridge is the Tower of London (0870 7566060), the famous historical 'royal fortress' that is home to the crown jewels, red-coated beefeaters and resident ravens.

⊖ Tower Hill

Map C **3**

Roman London

The City sits on the site of Londinium, the Roman capital of Britannia, and as such the area offers great potential for Roman-ruin spotting. After a visit to the splendid Museum of London (0870 4443852) where the full history of the capital from pre-Roman times to the present day is revealed through a fascinating series of interactive displays, head to nearby Bastion Highwalk for a glimpse at a segment of the original wall itself. Better still, the Guildhall Art Gallery (7332 3700) has over 4,000 pieces including remains of Londinium's original Roman amphitheatre, dating from the second century AD, which were found on the site in 1988.

Map C **4**

If you only do one thing in...
The City

Go to St Paul's Cathedral and try out the acoustics in the dome's Whispering Gallery (p.50) – if you can hear yourself above the din.

Best for...

Eating: Sample rich delights at the Gaucho Grill in the old vaults of the Bank of England (p.162).

Drinking: They may be not be as slick as your modern-day wine bar, but some of London's oldest pubs can be found on Fleet Street, including The Coach and Horses (p.164).

Sightseeing: Hop on one of only two remaining Routemaster bus services in London, the number 15 from Tower Hill to Trafalgar Square, and take in the sights from the top deck.

Shopping: Wander round Old Spitalfields Market, especially on a Sunday when the stalls are alive with a mix of quirky clothes and gifts (p.135).

Outdoor: Take a walk across Tower Bridge and stop to sample the view across the Thames.

South Bank

Once an unappealing, unloved poor relation of the fashionable areas of central London to the north, the South Bank now more than holds its own, boasting cultural activities galore and arguably the modern capital's most famous icon.

A decade or so ago, there wasn't much to draw visitors to the southern bank of the Thames, unless they were students of urban decay. But now, the mile and a half walk from Tower Bridge to Waterloo is a parade of arts, culture and entertainment. Along this stretch you'll find the Tate Modern and the London Eye, Shakespeare's Globe and the National Film Theatre. During the summer the South Bank really comes into its own thanks to the splendid river views and street festivals that draw crowds in their thousands. The London Film Festival, usually held in October/November, also brings a buzz to the bank. While the majority of the red-carpet glamour takes place in Leicester Square, there are various screenings and events held at the National Film Theatre in the Southbank Centre that are definitely worth checking out. The South Bank has also become a favourite spot for foodies with a good selection of restaurants, cafes and bars with alfresco areas in pretty, cobbled settings.

For **restaurants and bars** in the area, see p.168.

South Bank

Clink Prison Museum
Rail Br
Southwark Cathedral
Clink St
Bank End
Guy's Hospital
Stoney St
Tabard St
Great Dover St
Harper Rd
New Kent Rd
Elephant & Castle

Borough Market 5

Southwark St
Borough High St

Shakespeare's Globe 4
Tate Modern
Bankside Art Gallery
Hopton Almshouse

SOUTHWARK

THE BOROUGH

South Bank University

Blackfriars Rd
Southwark

Peabody Square

The Young Vic Theatre
Old Vic Theatre
Waterloo Rd

St George's Cathedral
Geraldine Mary Harmsworth Park

Imperial War Museum

LAMBETH

Oxo Tower
Gabriel's Wharf
The London Television Centre
National Theatre

SOUTH BANK

London Imax
Waterloo

Southbank Centre
Royal Festival Hall
Queen Elizabeth Hall, Purcell Room 3

Jubilee Gardens
London Eye 2
Dali Universe
Saatchi Gallery
London Aquarium 1
County Hall

Shell Centre

Lambeth North
Police Station
Kennington Rd

Florence Nightingale Museum
St Thomas' Hospital
United Dental & Medical Schools

Archbishop's Park
Lambeth Palace

Westminster Bridge

Cleopatra's Needle
Festival Pier
Waterloo Bridge
Queen's Walk
Victoria Embankment

200m

N

D

London Aquarium

7967 8000
Westminster Bridge Rd, SE1   www.londonaquarium.co.uk

The city's aquarium, inside the old County Hall building next to the London Eye, displays one of Europe's largest exhibitions of global aquatic life. More than 350 species are divided into 14 zones, each of which simulates a different environment. The Pacific section, for example, is home to four species of shark and puffer fish, while mono glide through the mangrove zone. The touch pool is hugely popular – visitors are invited to stroke giant winged rays and other flat fish. A favourite time to visit is during feeding (generally on Mondays, Wednesdays and Fridays from 12:00 to 12:30) when divers plunge into the main Atlantic tank, while a programme of regular educational talks gives visitors the chance to learn more about the aquarium's commitment to conservation.

⇌ ⊖ Waterloo

Map D 1

London Eye

0870 9908883
Westminster Bridge Rd, SE1   www.londoneye.com

What was initially intended to be a temporary construction for part of the country's millennium celebrations has rapidly become the capital's most popular paid-for attraction, and looks set to remain a permanent landmark on the London skyline. The London Eye is the largest observation wheel in the world, attracting around 10,000 visitors every day, and its 32 sealed capsules can carry a combined total of up to 800 passengers per half-hour revolution. But for all the remarkable statistics, what really impresses about the Eye is its sheer, joyful beauty. On a clear day you can see as far as Windsor Castle, almost 25 miles away, while its stylish curve and graceful action has quickly come to represent all that is forward-thinking about the city. If you're really clever the best time to go is just before dusk so that you get both a day and night view, just allow time for the queue. ⇌ ⊖ Waterloo

Map D **2**

Southbank Centre
Belvedere Rd, SE1

0870 3804300
www.southbankcentre.org.uk

The sharp concrete lines of brutal 1960s architecture make the Southbank Centre hard to miss, and have been the focus of much controversy over the decades. But the general livening up of the South Bank area, including the run of restaurants, bars and cafes that now line the riverbank, have brought the one thing that was needed to soften the area's harsh architecture – people. It is home to the National Theatre, Hayward Gallery and the recently renovated Royal Festival Hall, and also houses the National Film Theatre, one of London's best cinemas. Outside, people enjoy the riverside cafes and restaurants (there are few better places to go for a coffee or wine on a summer's day than the benches outside the NFT cafe), browse the interesting second-hand book market and take in the street performances as skateboarders show off their stuff underneath the complex's tiers and ramps. Thanks to the redevelopment and investment in this part of town, there is a much more vibrant atmosphere here. ⇌ ⊖ Waterloo

Map D **3**

Bankside

Stretching from Blackfriars Bridge to London Bridge is Bankside, a regenerated area of riverside cafes, restaurants and bars, plus three relatively new attractions – the Tate Modern gallery, Shakespeare's Globe and the Millenium Bridge. The Tate Modern (p.103) is a striking temple to contemporary art, converted from a disused power station, that looms large over the Thames. The Millennium Bridge, which spans the river directly outside the Tate, was the first new footbridge to be built across the Thames in over a century, but had to be temporarily closed shortly after it opened in 2000 as it swayed when people started to walk across it. Even though that problem has long been resolved, Londoners still affectionately refer to it as the 'wobbly bridge'. Shakespeare's Globe (7902 1400), which opened in 1997, is here as well, faithfully recreating the experience of Elizabethan audiences – right down to the uncomfortable gallery seating (bring a cushion) and the cheap, standing-only 'bear pit' below. Further towards London Bridge, you'll find a replica of The Golden Hinde, explorer Sir Francis Drake's ship, along with eerie treasures such as The Clink Prison museum (7403 0900), the atmospheric 17th century Old Operating Theatre museum (7188 2679) and The London Dungeon (7403 7221).

Map D 4

Borough

Just behind Bankside to the east, in the shadow of the impressive Southwark Cathedral, is Borough Market, a collection of wholesale fruit and veg stalls that have been trading on this spot for centuries (see p.130). The recent boom in organic and 'real' food across Britain in the last few years has put Borough firmly on the foodie map – every Friday and Saturday the market teems with Londoners out to get their hands on some of the freshest and finest meat and produce in the capital. The atmospheric streets around the market have also proved a favourite with filmmakers, featuring in hits such as *Bridget Jones's Diary* and *Lock, Stock and Two Smoking Barrels*. Southwark Cathedral is also worth a visit, if only to escape the sights and sounds of the city for a few moments.

Map D 5

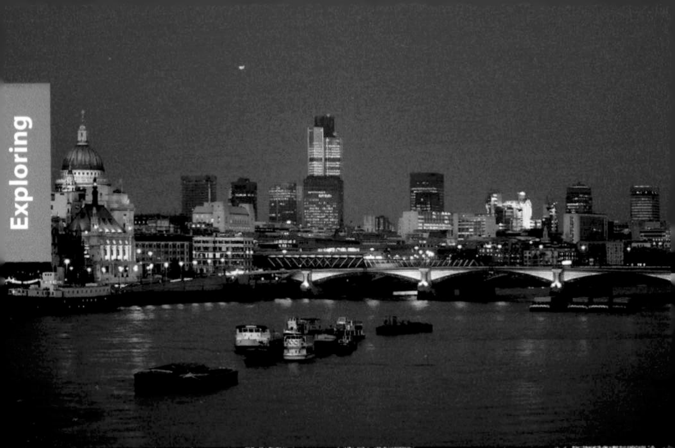

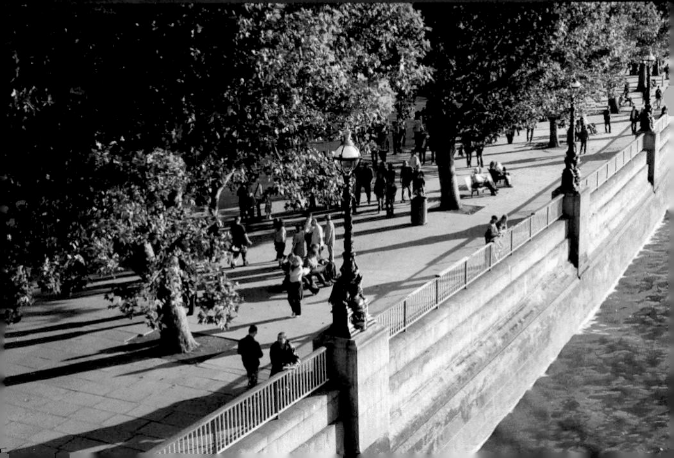

If you only do one thing in...
South Bank

Climb aboard one of the pods for a spectacular flight on the London Eye, the new icon of a 21st century capital.

Best for:

Eating: If you want to eat alfresco, Gabriel's Wharf is home to several different eateries in an attractive courtyard by the river.

Drinking: Sit and watch the world go by with a beer outside the NFT, or if lounge bars are your thing you'll be in your element at Home (p.165).

Sightseeing: Stroll along the South Bank from Waterloo Bridge to London Bridge (or vice versa) and take in the landmarks on both sides of the river.

Shopping: Borough Market on a Friday is a food shopper's delight – stock up on high quality fresh produce and cook yourself a treat (p.130).

Outdoor: See London from the water on an open-air boat tour from the South Bank, or jump on the Tate to Tate catamaran by the Millenium Bridge.

North London

From the manicured flower beds of Regent's Park to buzzing Islington, scruffy Camden and the positively rural Hamspitead Heath, north London encapsulates the variety that makes the capital so fascinating.

North London is defined by its open spaces. No other major world city can lay claim to a contained rural idyll like Hamspitead Heath, and sprawling green public spaces like Primrose Hill and Regent's Park. These areas become the city's garden in summer, but are just as beautiful after a fresh winter snowfall. But it can be urban here too – just look to the scruffy charms of Camden, or the sophistication of Islington. In terms of celebrity status north London is also home to a number of famous faces and a lazy summer afternoon in Hamstead Heath is sure to involve a bit of star spotting. When it comes to shopping, while the masses stick to the high streets of central London the informed get their fashion fix in the infamous Camden Market, and Islington has a growing number of boutiques. For many London residents the great north-south divide is a passionate debate, and the increasing number of eateries and drinking holes bestowed with a cool following here would make some believe that the north has just pipped the south in the race for social superiority.
*For **restaurants and bars** in the area, see p.172.*

British Library

7412 7332
www.bl.uk

96 Euston Rd, NW1

When the British Library moved to its new site at St Pancras in 1998 it marked the completion of the UK's largest building project of the 20th century. Housing a copy of every publication produced in the UK and Ireland, the British Library collection stands at around 150 million items and includes maps, magazines, music scores and patents as well as books. Treasures include the Magna Carta document, the recording of Nelson Mandela's trial speech, Beatles manuscripts and a Leonardo da Vinci notebook. The reading rooms are not open to casual visitors but the library welcomes guests into its exhibition galleries (which feature a permanent exhibition from the extensive collection in the Treasures Gallery along with a number of changing displays elsewhere), bookshop and lovely cafe and restaurant. ⇌ ⊖ King's Cross St Pancras

Hampstead Heath

7482 7073
www.cityoflondon.gov.uk

NW3

Hampstead Heath is one of north London's most treasured assets. Everyone who visits has a favourite feature, be it the views across London from Parliament Hill, the untamed beauty of its bathing ponds, the manicured lawns of the magnificent Kenwood House or simply the acres of semi-wild parkland freely available to be explored. One of the Heath's lesser-known treats is the Pergola and Hill Garden, an Edwardian walkway as long as Canary Wharf is tall, which offers wonderful views towards Harrow on the Hill. The traditional play area at Parliament Hill is a treat for children, and this part of the heath also boasts an outdoor lido and ice-skating rink (over the Christmas period). Regular walks and guided nature trails are organised throughout the year, and jazz concerts and fun fairs are some of the features of a full programme of summer events.

⊖ Highgate

Kenwood House

8348 1286

Hampstead Lane, NW3   www.english-heritage.org.uk

This beautiful neo-classical home sits majestically on the northern fringes of Hampstead Heath, and the combination of sumptuous interiors and stunning art makes it a London must-see. You can enjoy works by Rembrandt, Vermeer, Turner and Gainsborough, plus Constable's *Hampstead Heath with Pond and Bathers*, painted little more than a stone's throw away. One of the other great attractions of Kenwood is the grounds in which it sits. Beautifully landscaped, they offer visitors lakeside and woodland walks, while The Brew House Cafe (8348 2528) is a favourite spot for strollers to enjoy the hilltop views across London.

⊖ Golders Green

London Zoo

7722 3333

Regent's Park, NW1   www.londonzoo.com

The capital's main zoo is a popular year-round family attraction, although its central location can be the cause of the occasional surprise for passers by. In 2006, a dozen cheeky squirrel monkeys scaled the trees in their enclosure to freedom – much to the surprise of people strolling through Regent's Park. The zoo's animal checklist takes in all the big-name favourites, along with rarities such as Komodo dragons, the curious meerkats and charismatic penguins are perennially popular. London Zoo is a strong supporter of animal conservation and actively encourages visitors to get involved – you can even help by adopting an animal if you take a shine to one. ⊖ Camden Town

Lord's Cricket Ground
St John's Wood, W8

7616 8500
www.lords.org

Owned by the Marylebone Cricket Club (MCC), the 'spiritual home' of cricket is, in financial terms, also one of the most successful. It is the home of the England and Wales Cricket Board as well as the MCC Museum. The ground hosts npower Test matches and NatWest-sponsored one-day internationals, as well county championship matches (it's the home ground of Middlesex). Cricket fans can join a tour of the hallowed ground, taking in the famous Long Room in the pavilion and the original Ashes urn.

⊖ St John's Wood

Regent's Park
NW1

7486 7905
www.royalparks.gov.uk

Regent's Park is one of London's prettiest, designed by architect John Nash in 1811, and the perfect place for a summertime stroll. The stunning Queen Mary's Gardens and Rose Gardens (home to around 30,000 blooms of 400 varieties) are perfectly manicured treats, while areas of woodland and wildflowers continue to attract a wide variety of birdlife, for which the park is particularly famous. This carefully landscaped patch of green on the north of central

London also offers the largest outdoor sports area in the capital, with almost a quarter of the park's 410 acres made up of football pitches and facilities for tennis, netball, and golf coaching. The park is one of London's top venues for outdoor summer concerts, featuring everything from Shakespeare in the park at the Open Air Theatre (0870 0601811) to puppet shows and lunchtime and evening concerts in its bandstands.

⊖ Regent's Park

Camden

To the north-east of well-kept Regent's Park is the rather more scruffy Camden. The famous Camden Market (see p.133) is a hive of activity on weekends, when a mostly young crowd, made up of goths, indie kids and rockers, swarm the area around Camden Town tube station and nearby Stables Market, picking at the Doc Martens, antiques and bric-a-brac, or hunting out a bargain at the various classic vintage clothing emporia. Besides the shopping, Camden is also home to an energetic music scene, whether one-off gigs, DJ nights or regular live music. Venues such as Dublin Castle nurtured much of the city's music talent – The Buzzcocks and The Clash both played there, and it's where Madness got their big break – while the Jazz Cafe (7916 6060), Barfly (p.440), and recently revamped Roundhouse (7424 9991) are all key London venues. The Jazz Cafe is a great spot for the unconvential, as well as a few mainstream names, so when in town give them a call and check out their eclectic line-up. It's still possible to get away from the crowds however – the quiet calm of Regent's Canal, accessed via the bridges over Camden

Lock, is only moments away. While Camden certainly has its fair share of drifters and dwellers (and daytime drinkers) it has a unique charm that attracts a truly mix-and-match crowd, and whether you want to spend pennies or pounds it can be done on Camden's streets.

Islington

Drinkers, diners and shoppers are all drawn to Islington by the magnet that is Upper Street. This major thoroughfare runs the length of the area, from Angel tube to Highbury & Islington, and moves with a bustle to rival that of Oxford Street. Towards Angel, Upper Street is home to supermarkets, chain stores, bawdy late-night boozers and the pleasingly chaotic Chapel Market, near Liverpool Road. Just off Upper Street to the east is Camden Passage, a discreet collection of boutiques, antique shops and home to a great collectibles market on weekends. Beyond Islington Green, things become more refined. Boutiques and quirky furnishing stores nestle alongside treasures such as The Hart Gallery (7704 1131), showcasing modern paintings, sculptures and ceramics, and two feted independent theatres, the intimate King's Head (see p.174), part of the pub of the same name, and the Almeida (7359 4404), which attracts top international actors. Off to the east is Canonbury, a pretty, exclusive enclave that's one of London's most sought-after addresses, and boasts a number of famous former residences – take a wander around and look out for the Blue Plaque at 17a Canonbury Square, marking the house where social satirist Evelyn Waugh once lived.

If you only do one thing in...
North London

Enjoy some countryside in the city – spend a morning rambling through Hampstead Heath, pausing to drink in the views of central London from the Brew House Café at Kenwood House.

Best for...

Eating: There's an almost endless choice of cuisines along Islington's Upper Street.

Drinking: Sip a classic cocktail at Cuba Libre (p.172) and enjoy a taste of the Caribbean, from the music to the tapas.

Sightseeing: Go wild at London Zoo – polar bears, penguins, meerkats and monkeys can all be found in the north-east corner of Regent's Park.

Shopping: Get kitted out with the goths and rockers at the clothing emporium in Camden Market (p.133).

Outdoor: All the world's a stage – especially Regent's Park, where you can watch Shakespeare under the stars at the magnificent Open Air Theatre (p.65).

East London

The old East End has a gritty urban history, from suffering under the Blitz to Jack the Ripper and the Krays, and is now re-inventing itself as the new heart of the city's creative industries.

East London has given the world the enduring image of the chirpy cockney, and possibly the most infamous serial killer. But modern east london is unrecognisable from that of even 10 years ago. Spilling out from the City is the heart of London's Bangladeshi community, buzzing markets, artistic collectives and food and drink options unlike any other part of town. Head further south and see what the world sets its watch by. *For restaurants and bars in the area, see p.184.*

Dennis Severs' House

7247 4013
18 Folgate St, E1   www.dennissevershouse.co.uk

Artist Dennis Severs, who died in 1999, transformed his London residence into a re-creation of an early 18th century home, creating a 'living museum'. The 10 rooms, each lit by fire and candle, are wonderfully atmospheric; food smells trip the senses, while the creaking of stairways and chiming of clocks all add to the feeling that this is a house in which people actually live. It's a long way from the studied formality of the city's other historic houses, but if what you're after is a glimpse into a forgotten world, look no further. Opening times are restricted to Monday evenings, and in the afternoon on the first and third Sunday and subsequent Monday of each month. Reservations are necessary for Monday evening tours.

≥ ⊖ Liverpool Street

Eltham Palace

8294 2548
www.elthampalace.org.uk

Court Yard, SE9

Eltham Palace is one of the capital's most extraordinary historic houses. The first royal owner was Edward II in the early 14th century, and it was continuously remodelled and extended into one of the kingdom's largest palaces. Despite such heritage (Henry VIII grew up here) the building fell into decline in the 17th century, and remained that way until it was bought by Stephen and Virginia Courtauld in 1933. The pair restored the Great Hall to its former glory, and built an adjoining art deco home for themselves featuring a lavish circular ocean-liner-styled central room with luxury furnishings. The brilliantly preserved result is a stunning evocation of 1930s London, charmingly juxtaposed against the grandeur of the medieval palace. The buildings are set in 19 acres of gardens, which surround the original moat and offer great views over London – perfect for a picnic on a hot summer's day. ≥ Eltham

Greenwich

Stepping off the train or boat here is rather like entering another world – or another London, at least. This pretty, green neighbourhood is the birthplace of Greenwich Mean Time, a Unesco World Heritage Site, boasts hundreds of acres of glorious parkland, and is steeped in maritime history.

Highlights within Greenwich Park itself include the Royal Observatory and the National Maritime Museum (see p.99), and lesser-known attractions such as Ranger's House (8853 0035). This elegant Georgian villa now houses the Wernher Collection – a wonderful anthology of over 700 pieces of medieval and renaissance works of art. The area's other big maritime attraction is the Cutty Sark (8858 3445), a former tea clipper that last sailed commercially in 1922. Currently closed for renovations, the ship will reopen in late 2008, but until then there is a temporary exhibition nearby.

The main shopping area around Greenwich Church Street is a great place to browse independent boutiques, but the real retail draw around these parts is Greenwich Market, selling handicrafts, clothing, collectables and antiques. It's open throughout the week, but really comes alive on weekends.

Shoreditch

An influx of artists seeking cheap studio space saw the former East End slums of Shoreditch soar in popularity in the late 90s. While rising prices have meant much of the early art community has moved on, Shoreditch is still a great area to visit. A good place to start any tour is Hoxton Square. It is leafy but slightly down at heel, and on a warm summer evening it still fills with more fashionable young things than you can shake a paintbrush at. It was once the axis around which Shoreditch's new cool swung and is home to the most famous of 'britart' galleries, White Cube (7930 5373). Two other excellent contemporary art spaces nearby are Victoria Miro (7336 8109) and Flowers East (7920 7777). For a more traditional flavour of Shoreditch, visit the bustling Hoxton Street Market, located on a stretch of road also home to authentic pie and mash shop, F Cooke. Nearby Hoxton Hall (7684 0060) is a traditional Victorian music hall and the only one of its kind still operating today.

Spitalfields

The area around Spitalfields and Brick Lane is undergoing a similar transformation to its fashionable neighbour Shoreditch. Nowhere is this more clearly seen than Old Spitalfields Market (see p.135), where you can buy organic vegetables, designer clothes, and everything in between. Sunday is the most vibrant day for a visit, which is also the best time to experience the area's other two hugely popular markets – the Columbia Road Flower Market (see p.135) and the northern end of nearby Brick Lane (p.132), which offers up goods ranging from old records to new shoes.

Spitalfields lies in the shadow of the striking Christ Church, and the area is currently best-known for its buzzing Bangladeshi community and the run of curry houses in and around Brick Lane. Shoreditch has a long history of immigrant communities, including French Huguenots and Jews. The Museum of Immigration and Diversity (7247 5352) on Princelet Street aims to tell that history. Phone ahead as there is limited access. Sticking with the past, the eccentric Dennis Severs' House is a self-styled 'living museum,' and the notorious Ten Bells pub opposite Spitalfields market on Commercial Street was reputedly frequented by Jack the Ripper and his victims.

If you only do one thing in...
East London

Get a slice of Asia in London at Brick Lane, otherwise known as Banglatown. Best visited on Sunday for a morning bagel and a cheap curry lunch, divided by a walk round the market (p.132).

Best for...

Eating: When in the East End, do as the cockneys do – tuck in to some pie and mash (and a jellied eel, if you can stomach it) from F Cooke (p.73).

Drinking: Head to Hoxton Square for a tipple with the trendy set – if you're cool enough, that is.

Sightseeing: Enter the dark world of the Victorian East End on a tour of Jack the Ripper's many haunts, followed by a night cruise down the Thames (p.91).

Shopping: Hand-crafted gifts and quirky clothing are all under one roof at Old Spitalfields Market (p.135).

Outdoor: Lose track of time at the home of time in the wide open spaces of glorious Greenwich Park (p.71).

South London

South-west London has been the more exclusive end of town for many years, a fact clearly evident in the grand houses of Knightsbridge and Chelsea, and grandiose Victorian institutions and monuments in South Kensington.

South London - and the south-west in particular - is a picturesque scene of leafy loveliness, defined by its green spaces as much as the north. It has benefited from Victorian philanthropy perhaps more than any other part of the city, with its botanic gardens, wetlands reserve, public spaces and impressive institutions dedicated to advancing public knowledge and understanding of nature and science.

*For **restaurants and bars** in the area, see p.176.*

Kew Gardens

TW9

8332 5655
www.rbgkew.org.uk

While not strictly a nature reserve, the Royal Botanic Gardens (to use Kew's proper name) is recognised as one of the leading plant conservation centres in the world. Many of its botanical specimens were planted in the 17th and 18th centuries and much of the centre's ongoing research focuses on this extraordinary collection. Wildlife and conservation areas include a bee garden, a stag beetle loggery, a biodiversity garden and rare native trees. Visit in spring to see the woodland floor become a lush carpet of bluebells, snowdrops and wild garlic. There are formal gardens too, including rose, Japanese and rock gardens, while the iconic glass-and-steel Victorian Palm House is recognised as one of the finest structures of its kind. ⊖ Kew

London Wetland Centre

8409 4400

Queen Elizabeth's Walk, SW13 www.wwt.org.uk

The London Wetland Centre is the only project of its kind in the world – a wild expanse of manmade wetlands in the heart of a capital city. It covers 40 spectacular acres and was created on a series of former reservoirs. Local birds and wildlife have taken to it like ducks to water – in 2006 four avocet chicks hatched in the centre, a rarity as these birds tend not to breed inland. The modern visitor centre offers vast expanses of glass windows through which you can see the 180 species of wild birds. Top spots include peregrine falcons and a breeding colony of sand martins, along with more than half the UK's species of dragonfly and eight species of bat. ⇌ Barnes

Richmond Park

8948 3209

TW9 www.royalparks.gov.uk

Richmond Park is London's largest Royal Park, and the site feels rather more like wild countryside than the carefully cultivated space of its counterparts in town. It's famous for its ancient oak trees and roaming deer, and you may even see parrots flying overhead. The park's sheer scale means that it's popular with sports enthusiasts too, the flat, wide expanse making it a great place for informal kickabouts among groups of picnickers.

There are some great stretches of road for cyclists and bike hire is available year-round from the Roehampton Gate car park (7581 1188), would-be anglers can buy a fishing permit (8948 3209) and try their luck at Pen Ponds, or there's a 'pay and play' 18 hole golf course and driving range (8876 3205).

⇄ ⊖ Richmond

Chelsea

King's Road is one of the capital's most iconic thoroughfares. The centre of 'Swinging London' in the 1960s and punk in the 1970s, its special mix of bohemia and wealth has long been part of its attraction. While a visit to King's Road no longer holds such cultural sway, it still affords a splendid opportunity to peek into the area's social past. The array of English Heritage Blue Plaques cladding its shopfronts and houses includes *Rule Britannia* composer Thomas Arne at 215, while 19th century pre-Raphaelite artist Dante Gabriel Rossetti once lived at

nearby Cheyne Walk, the exclusive strip of riverfront housing that was more recently home to Mick Jagger. Neighbouring Knightsbridge is where you'll find some of London's most exclusive shopping, particularly Harrods and the fashion stores of Sloane Street. On the banks of the Thames, the grounds of the Wren-designed Royal Hospital Chelsea play host to the annual Chelsea Flower Show in May, while visitors at other times of the year can explore its courtyards, chapel and hall for free, or pop into the onsite National Army Museum (7881 2455). A short stroll away you'll also find one of London's best-kept secrets, the delightful Chelsea Physic Garden (7352 5646), which was set up to study the benefits of botany in relation to medicine, and is a wonderful place for a summer afternoon.

South Kensington

South Kensington is a living monument to the pioneering institutions of the Victorian era and Britain's empirical pomp. Perched at the far corner of Kensington Gardens, is the golden, gothic spire of the George Gilbert Scott-designed Albert Memorial. The main attractions here are the Natural History Museum, the Science Museum and the Victoria & Albert Museum, (see p.102). North of this famous trio is the rotund Royal Albert Hall (7589 8212), home of the Proms and around which you can take a tour, while on the opposite side of the road, just inside Kensington Gardens, is the Albert Memorial, a lavish, ornate tribute commissioned by Queen Victoria in honour of her late husband and finished in 1872. In the streets behind the Albert Memorial lie educational institutions such as the Royal College of Music.

If you only do one thing in...
South London

See the world-famous Royal Botanic Gardens at Kew, a stunning collection of plants and flowers from around the globe (p.76).

Best for...

Eating: Once famous for fashion and music, King's Road in Chelsea is now home to some first-rate restaurants and cafes.

Drinking: From posh to mosh, get down and dirty in The Fridge, the infamous Brixton club (p.179).

Sightseeing: Not one, not two, but three of the world's best museums, all in one small area of South Kensington – a must for every visitor (p.79).

Shopping: If you've got cash to splash, head to Knightsbridge for Harrods (p.136) and Harvey Nics (p.139) and big-name fashion on Sloane Street.

Outdoor: Take a stroll round the delightful Richmond Park, south London's very own wilderness, complete with roaming deer (p.77).

West London

Rich with leafy grandeur, fashion conscious locals and abundant multiculturalism, west London has long been one of the most desirable parts of the capital to visit.

This is the smart part of town, where royals live and go out to play. It hosts palaces and parks, and some grand old houses in its swanky residential areas. West London is also where you'll find Notting Hill, home to politicians, film makers, and the world's largest street carnival after Rio. It can often be missed by tourists that get stuck on the main sights in town, but is well worth exploring. *For restaurants and bars in the area, see p.180.*

Apsley House

149 Piccadilly, W1

7499 5676
www.english-heritage.org.uk/apsleyhouse

Also known as 'Number One London' because it was the first building encountered after passing through the toll gates at the top of Knightsbridge, Apsley House was the home of the first Duke of Wellington. His descendents remain in residence today, making it the capital's last great aristocratic townhouse still in use. This neo-classical mansion houses the Duke's collection of furniture, silver, porcelain, medals and memorabilia. The art display contains works by European masters such as Velazquez, Rubens and Goya, plus important British paintings. Wellington moved into the house in 1817, two years after his victory at the Battle of Waterloo – so unsurprisingly Napoleon looms large in the collections. Along with the sumptuous Sevres Egyptian dinner service, designed by the French general for his wife Josephine, there is also a colossal nude sculpture of Napoleon by Canova. You can buy a ticket that gives access to neighbouring Wellington Arch, which offers magnificent views over the Houses of Parliament and Hyde Park. ⊖ Hyde Park Corner

Hyde Park & Kensington Gardens
W2

7298 2100
www.royalparks.gov.uk

Hyde Park offers 350 acres of landscaped gardens in which to watch wildlife, ride horses, rollerblade and row, and also frequently hosts concerts, rallies and events (in 2005 it staged its biggest performance to date: the Live 8 charity concert). Elsewhere, Speakers' Corner, near Marble Arch, has been a 'cradle of free speech' since 1866, drawing crowds every Sunday morning as ordinary citizens have their say, while the Serpentine has proved popular for sunbathing and swimming since 1930. Other highlights include the Serpentine Gallery, and the Albert Memorial in neighbouring Kensington Gardens, which backs on to the palace in which Princess Diana lived. Indeed, Kensington Gardens and Hyde Park have become synonymous with the late princess. The Diana Memorial Fountain pays tribute to her memory, attracting around one million visitors a year, while the seven mile Diana Memorial Walk follows a trail through Kensington Gardens, Hyde Park and St James's Park.

⊖ Hyde Park Corner/High Street Kensington

Kensington Palace

W2

0870 7515170
www.kensington-palace.org.uk

When Princess Diana died in 1997, the focus of the world's media turned to Kensington Palace, her residence since her marriage to Prince Charles in 1981 (and subsequent divorce), as thousands turned out to mourn by the palace gates. Floral tributes are still frequently left today, and its significance as a site of memorial to Diana continues. Beautifully located in Kensington Gardens, the former Jacobean mansion has been a favoured home of English royalty for centuries. Queen Victoria was born here, and she first opened the state apartments to the public on her 80th birthday in 1898. It's a tradition of access that has remained intact, on and off, ever since. Visitors can also see the charming royal ceremonial dress collection, featuring items worn by Queen Elizabeth II and Princess Diana. Other highlights include The Orangery and pretty sunken garden. Open daily.

⊖ High Street Kensington

Little Venice

Little Venice is an oasis in the heart of London, tucked away in the otherwise largely residential Maida Vale. Officially occupying the relatively small basin where the Grand Union and Regent's canals meet at the junction of Westbourne Terrace Road and Blomfield Road, this pretty area of water is home to a number of barges and narrowboats, including a cafe, gallery and, in the winter, a children's puppet theatre (7249 6876). It's perfect for a weekend stroll – five minutes west leads you to the fashionable Waterway pub (7266

3557), while the journey east makes a really nice hour's walk through to Regent's Park and Camden.

Notting Hill

North-west of Hyde Park lies west London's most well-known residential area, Notting Hill – famous for its annual carnival, Portobello Road Market and impressive white-fronted houses, and of course the film of the same name. (Look for the famous blue door if you're a real film trivia buff). The colourful carnival, a celebration of London's Afro-Caribbean culture, takes place every August bank holiday weekend, and the parade runs along Ladbroke Grove, Notting Hill's spine. In recent years there have been some problems with crowds during carnival, so it's best to leave before the sun does. There's another street in the area, however, that is even more well-known, and a little more sophisticated . Portobello Road (where a struggling George Orwell once lived in a bedsit at number 22) is home to the weekly antiques and bric-a-brac market, and is packed solid every Saturday (see p.135). For a quieter alternative, consider visiting on a Friday for the market that takes place directly opposite a run of tasty, cheap eateries, including the splendid S&M Café – that's sausage and mash – under the Westway. If you want to try a bit of star-spotting, have a mooch around the boutiques and restaurants at the top end of Westbourne Grove and Ledbury Road, which are considerably more upmarket. On any given day you could be sharing aisle space with A-listers, from Gwyneth Paltrow, Kate Moss and Stella McCartney to local Nobel prize-winning author Harold Pinter.

If you only do one thing in...
West London

Strap on some wheels from Slick Willies hire shop
(www.slickwillies.co.uk) and join the rollerblading roll
call around Hyde Park.

Best for...
Eating: When you've tired yourself out shopping,
there's plenty of fine nosh on offer in Notting Hill to
help regain some energy.

Drinking: Sample the live music at The Castle with
a pint of ale in this wonderfully shabby pub (p.182).

Sightseeing: If you've got something you want to
get off your chest, or fancy listening to someone
else do it for you, then the irate throng at Hyde
Park's Speaker's Corner is not to be missed (p.83).

Shopping: Share aisle space with A-list nannies in
the upmarket shops of Westbourne Grove.

Outdoor: Take a stroll along the canals at Little
Venice for a glimpse at two very different ways of
life – riverboat residents on the water and million-
aire mansions on dry land.

Tours

An organised tour is a great way to experience the best of London's attractions. Whether by cab, bike, bus, boat, air or on foot, you're sure to find an interesting tour that will show you all the sights.

Black Taxi Tours of London

7935 9363

Various locations · www.blacktaxitours.co.uk

London cabbies are famous for knowing the streets of London like the back of their hand, so who better to show you around? They offer general sightseeing tours, plus special tours such as Secret London or Tales of the Thames. You can also customise your own outing. Two-hour tours cost £85 (good for up to five passengers), with a £5 supplement on weekends and bank holidays.

The London Bicycle Tour Company

7928 6838

SE1 · www.londonbicycle.com

Located on the South Bank for instant access to the Thames path, this company gives cyclists the option of pedalling their way through one of three half-day guided tours of the capital's attractions, or just hiring a bike and going it alone. Either way getting 'on yer bike' is a great way to explore London's streets. The tours cost £14.95, and bicycle hire is from £2.50 per hour.

Catamaran Cruises

WC2

7987 1185

www.catamarancruisers.co.uk

Circular boat-tours depart every 15 minutes from Waterloo, Embankment, Bankside, Tower and Greenwich piers. If you want to make an evening of it, try a dinner cruise – it's a lovely, romantic way to see the city by night. Circular tours cost £9 for adults, and dinner trips start at £69.

Circular Cruises

SW1

7839 2111

A hop-on, hop-off boat tour that sails from Westminster or Festival Pier (summer only) to St Katharine Dock, near Tower Bridge. Services and running times alter according to the season so be sure to check before setting out. A one-day adult ticket costs £7.

Capital Limo

Various locations

7839 2111

www.capitallimoco.uk

For a truly decadent experience get yourself a limo for £195 and enjoy a three-hour city tour in style.

London Duck Tours

SE1

7928 3132

www.londonducktours.co.uk

A tour aboard this bright yellow amphibious vehicle (originally used to take the troops ashore on the 1944 D-Day landings) is the perfect way to see London by road and water without having to leave your seat. The transition from dry land to the River Thames is great fun too. Tours cost £17.50 for adults and £12.00 for kids aged 12 and under.

Big Bus Tours

7233 9533

Various locations — www.bigbustours.com

A 24 hour hop-on, hop-off ticket on one of these open-top double-decker sightseeing tours costs £20. There are two interchangeable routes, and the fare includes a river cruise and guided walking tours. Fast-track attraction tickets are also available. Get on at Paddington Station, Marble Arch, Green Park, Victoria and Trafalgar Square.

Evan Evans Tours

7950 1777

Various locations — www.evanevanstours.co.uk

This long-established tour company offers three London sightseeing trips in luxury coaches, led by a qualified Blue Badge guide. A full-day tour of the best of the capital's attractions, complete with river cruise and a pub lunch, costs from £65 per person. Half-day tours are available from £28.

The Original London Sightseeing Tour

8877 1722

Various locations

www.theoriginaltour.com

You can buy your tickets on the day for this hop-on, hop-off service, or book online with a discount. Buses leave

Show Us Your Badge

If you're considering joining a tour or hiring a private guide, it's worth checking if they carry a Blue Badge – this means that they are officially registered, have received proper training and should know the city inside out. There are more than 1,000 operating in London (see www.blue-badge.org.uk).

Buses leave every 10-20 minutes from Baker Street, Piccadilly Circus, Marble Arch, Victoria and Embankment Pier, and include a free river cruise. Tickets are valid for 24 hours from first use. The on-the-day fare is £18 for adults.

Premium Tours
WC1   7404 5100
                          www.premiumtours.co.uk

Premium offer bespoke bus excursions, including a Jack the Ripper tour which takes you through the Victorian murderer's East End haunts followed by a Thames 'terror cruise' at night. Adults tickets are £19.50. Other itineraries include a half-day visit to the capital's top royal attractions (£35), with a private guided tour of the Tower of London.

Walking Tours

A walking tour is a fun way to explore the capital at a more relaxed pace. Whatever your area of interest, there's a good chance that someone, somewhere has designed a walk that will appeal to you. You can join a guided tour, or choose to go it alone and be your own tour guide. Just make sure you're wearing comfortable shoes.

Guided Walking Tours

Original London Walks (7624 3978) is one of the capital's most established walking tour companies, and offers a huge range of itineraries. Whether it's exploring areas such as Mayfair and Little Venice, ghost tours or tracing the old haunts of notables from The Beatles to Jack the Ripper, it's all covered. If the dark and ghoulish side of London is your thing, TV historian Richard Jones also runs Jack the Ripper and ghost tours (8530 8443). City Secrets Walks does spooky tours too, as well as a very good guide to Shakespeare's Elizabethan London (7625 5155). The similarly named Secret London (8881 2933) offers insightful explorations of different parts of town, as well as theatrical, legal and film-themed tours. For a specialist movie-related expedition join film historian Sandra Shevey's tour of locations used in Alfred Hitchcock pictures.

Self-Guided Walking Tours

If you'd prefer to stride out on your own, there are several self-guided options to get you around town. Pick up a free London Wall Walk leaflet from the Museum of London, which will guide you through a two-mile tour of the old Roman wall that once encircled the ancient city of Londinium. The Jubilee Walkway is a 14 mile self-guided walk originally created in honour of the Queen's Silver Jubilee in 1977, and extended and updated for her Golden Jubilee in 2002. There are five central London itineraries in total, each dotted with plaques acknowledging important sites along the way. Leaflets are available at www.jubileewalkway.com or from Tourist Information offices. Another plaque-based option is to tour around some of the 800 or so English Heritage 'Blue Plaques' that adorn many of the capital's private residences, marking former homes of famous or notable people. You can design your own walk at www.english-heritage.org.uk/blueplaques or get hold of a guidebook from most bookshops. If you'd like to escape to the water, London's canals offer tranquil settings with great views and a fascinating history. Download one of British Waterways' free walking guides from www.waterscape.com/londonwalks and explore London along the banks of its historic canals. If you fancy a bicycle self-guided tour check out Capital Sport (01296 631671, www.capital-sport.co.uk), which allows you to explore London, as well as escape the city, on wheels.

A Full Calendar

There's no 'best season' to visit London. On top of its year-round attractions, you'll find a full calendar of special events. From outdoor ice rinks in winter to blooming flowers at Kew and Chelsea in spring, the Notting Hill Carnival in the summer and proms in autumn, there are always events to entertain you.

Arts & Culture

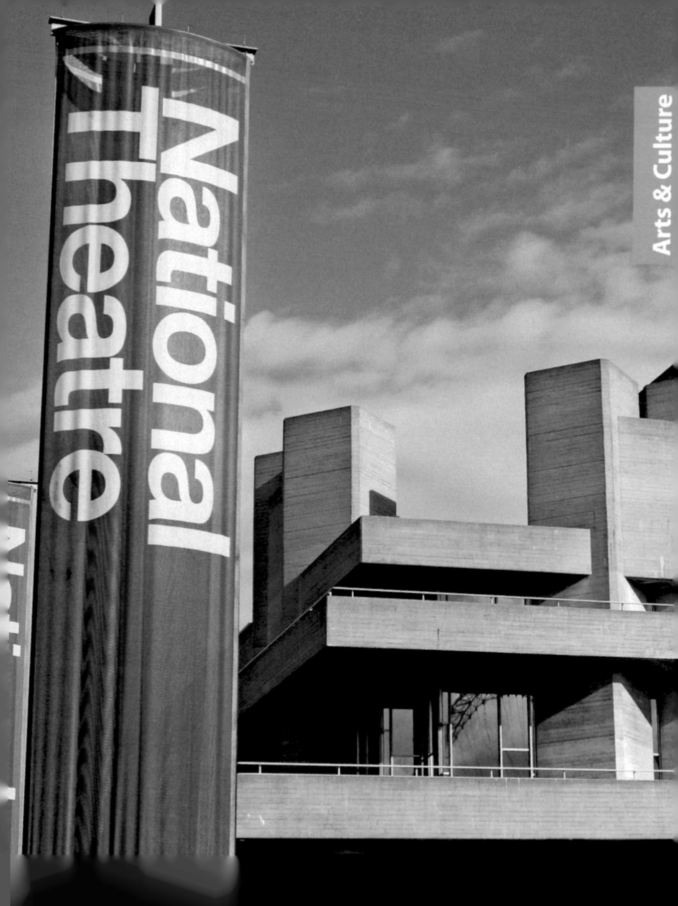
National Theatre

Arts & Entertainment

Whether you want to expand your knowledge in one of the capital's many museums or have your ribs tickled at a comedy club, it's all on offer in London.

A roll call of top cultural attractions combined with a gleeful range of niche entertainment means London rewards people clutching a detailed itinerary as well as those happy to pitch up and see what takes their fancy on the day.

Special exhibitions excepted, entrance to London's major public museums and galleries is free – it won't cost you a penny to get into the South Ken trio, the Tates, National Gallery, National Portrait Gallery, British Museum or the Imperial War Museum, although you can make a donation.

You'll never be faced with the prospect of having nothing to do in London, but if your stay is a short one, tough choices will need to be made about what to fit in. Being over-ambitious may lead to a pounding head, sore feet and grumpy companions. A good idea is to limit yourself geographically, and choose your destinations wisely to maintain interest levels.

The Natural History Museum, Science Museum and V&A are conveniently close together, but it takes a hardy soul to do all three in one day – and kids will find such museum-hopping particularly hard-going. It's best to explore thoroughly the one you find most appealing, and scoot into the others to visit a couple of exhibits or have coffee.

Choices are plentiful too for evening entertainment. Those eyeing a particular show should check out the ticket situation in advance or risk disappointment. A handful of venues, such as the Royal National Theatre, hold back some tickets until the day of performance, but many plays, operas and concerts need to be booked well in advance (although Leicester Square's half-price theatre ticket booths are always worth a try).

Watching a film is an option that can fairly safely be left to the last minute. Comedy and cabaret clubs and music pubs rarely sell out, but queues form at the better known venues.

Museums & Galleries

Renaissance painters compete with Britart badboys for the attention of art enthusiasts, while museum-hoppers can happily lose hours and even days in London's world-famous institutions.

British Museum

Great Russell St, WC1   7323 8299

With more than 90 galleries and one of the world's foremost collections of antiquities, spanning ancient Egypt, Greece, early Britain and more, a visit to the British Museum can easily take up a whole day – or you can pop in for an hour to tick off the Rosetta Stone and the controversial Elgin Marbles. Housed in a spectacular Victorian take on classic Greek architecture, the interior Great Court of the museum was redesigned recently to incorporate a striking glass-and-metal latticed dome, creating the largest covered square in Europe and a great spot to sip a coffee after you've soaked up some culture.

⊖ Russell Square

Design Museum

28 Shad Thames, SE1   0870 8339955

In the shadow of Tower Bridge, the Design Museum is housed in a modern glass-fronted building in sight of the City and Canary Wharf. Dedicated to 20th and 21st century product design, architecture and fashion, the gallery combines an upmarket sales showroom with serious exhibition space.

Despite the intellectual approach taken to design, the museum presents its knowledge with a light (and light-hearted) touch. While it's one of London's most interesting and innovative museums, it's not the largest – half a day is enough time to explore. A 'design action pack', complete with fun treasure trails, should keep the youngsters amused.

⊖ Tower Hill

Imperial War Museum

Lambeth Rd, SE1   7416 5320

Serious as its subject matter is – the history of war in the 20th century – this museum succeeds in its quest to give a human face to its theme, with exhibitions that are both intelligent and thought-provoking. A special feature running until 2008 reviews the history, impact and effect of the second world war as it was experienced through the eyes of Britain's children, while there are warplanes and tanks for those that like that sort of thing. The permanent holocaust exhibition is a powerful yet restrained demonstration of Nazi persecution of Jews and other groups. ⊖ ≩ Waterloo

National Maritime Museum & Royal Observatory

Park Row, SE10   8858 4422

London's naval past is the focus of this museum, guaranteed to bring out the wannabe sailor in you and the perfect place to kick off an exploration of the period charms of Maritime Greenwich, a Unesco World Heritage site. One of the largest collections of boats and navigational equipment in the world is complemented by the star-gazing gadgets of the Royal

Observatory, and the museum's location as home of the Prime Meridian allows visitors to take pictures of themselves straddling the eastern and western hemispheres. Also on site is Queen's House, home to a fine art collection, with the Cutty Sark tea clipper, built in 1869 and now permanently housed in dry dock, a short stroll away. **DLR** Cutty Sark

Natural History Museum
Cromwell Rd, SW7   7942 5000

The world-famous dinosaur exhibitions tend to top most people's must-see list at this South Kensington museum, and the sight of a full-sized diplodocus skeleton flooded by natural light from the ceiling of the cathedral-like interior of the museum's central hall is one to cherish. The ever-popular dinosaur exhibits apart, there's more for visitors to explore and enjoy, from life-size models of sea creatures to the spectacular Earth Galleries, which include a horribly realistic simulation of an earthquake. After that, retire to the serene haven that is the Wildlife Centre, a garden in the heart of the museum that opens during the summer months.

⊖ South Kensington

Science Museum
Exhibition Rd, SW7   0870 8704868

The Science Museum was set up in 1857 after profits from the Great Exhibition earlier that decade were used to purchase land in South Kensington to build institutions dedicated to the emerging fields of science and technology. From early locomotives Stephenson's Rocket and Puffing Billy to Crick and Watson's model of DNA, scientific history and contemporary developments are generously covered. The building's classical interior incorporates glass lifts and all the mod cons necessary for high-tech exhibition spaces, complete with hands-on educational fun to appeal to the kids – there's even science sleepovers for young Einsteins.

⊖ South Kensington

Sir John Soane's Museum

13 Lincoln's Inn Fields, WC2   7405 2107

The celebrated 18th century architect Sir John Soane bought this typical London townhouse with the intention of displaying his collection of art, antiquities and curios from around the globe, and planned before his death in 1837 that it would survive as a museum after he was gone. The result is a fascinatingly eclectic display offering not only a chance to see the collection, but an insight into the mind of a collector. Important works include paintings by Turner and Canaletto, plus Hogarth's famous satirical series *A Rake's Progress*. Equally fascinating are the smaller exhibits in the house's nooks and crannies – stained glass, timepieces and everyday domestic furniture from the early 19th century. ⊖ Holborn

Victoria & Albert Museum

Cromwell Rd, SW7   7942 2000

The third of South Kensington's 'big three', the V&A offers the most extensive collection of art and design in the world, with entire rooms dedicated to glassware and tapestry and others furnished to replicate a period style in detail. Visitors arrive via the Grand Entrance and approach an illuminated reception desk under the vast, Medusa-like coils of glass suspended from the striking domed ceiling. This clash of styles works beautifully and is a good metaphor for the museum itself.

⊖ South Kensington

Institute of Contemporary Art

The Mall, SE1   7930 0483

The lure of the ICA is much more than what's on the walls. Its setting, a stately Georgian terrace close to Buckingham Palace, provides a pleasing juxtaposition with its cutting-edge exhibitions, which have showcased the best of modern art, from Jackson Pollock to the Chapman brothers. With screens showing international indie cinema gems, an excellent bookshop and a cool cafe bar (with late licence), the venue draws an arty crowd every day of the week.

⊖⇌ Charing Cross

Tate Modern

Bankside, SE1   7887 8000

Housed in a former power station, the towering Tate hugs the Thames, offering postcard views of the skyline. Inside, the vast Turbine Hall stages special installations, which have included giant slides, piles of boxes and a radiant indoor sun. Elsewhere, its programme of talks and films, gallery shop and buzzy cafes ensure a constant stream of visitors. The art itself is a crash course in modern western work and blockbuster temporary exhibitions. Catch a catamaran to the Tate Britain over in Pimlico. ⊖⇌ Blackfriars

Film & Cinema

From *Dogme* to *Die Hard*, and film noir to blaxploitation, the capital's cinemas have something for every enthusiast of the big screen.

If you fancy jostling with the paparazzi to catch a glimpse of Hollywood's A-list, then head to Leicester Square, where the Empire and Odeon frequently host blockbuster premieres. If there's no star appearances on when you're in town, you can still go and see the latest movie on the venues' giant screens.

Away from the red carpet, you can catch the latest box office smashes at major cinema chains Cineworld, Vue and Odeon, which have outlets throughout the West End and beyond, although London offers much more than the mainstream for serious devotees of the silver screen.

The National Film Theatre on London's South Bank is a cineaste's dream sequence, with an imaginative programme of classics and cult favourites, talks and events. Less highbrow and just out of sight of the bright lights of Leicester Square, the quirky Prince Charles cinema is known for its refreshingly low ticket prices and flamboyant celebrations of camp classics – check out its infamous 'Sing-along-a Sound of Music' night.

The Curzon Soho on Shaftesbury Avenue has coffee and fancy cake upstairs and a laid-back bar downstairs to complement a menu of arthouse films. Tucked away in Bloomsbury's resurgent Brunswick Centre is the Renoir, another reliable choice for leftfield and world cinema in an easy-going atmosphere. Over in the City, the Barbican Cinema has an impressive main auditorium and an intimate small screen. The Screen chain, operating cosy cinemas at Islington Green, Haverstock Hill and Baker Street, is also popular with those hoping to avoid chattering teens and the whiff of hot dogs.

Despite the march of the multiplex, independent cinemas have carved out a niche in the capital and continue to hold their own. The indies are also your best bet for kids' cinema clubs, parent-and-baby screenings, film societies and quiz nights. In Dalston, the Rio is a popular local venue showing the more interesting of the latest releases and offering special showings of children's classics and world cinema. The Ritzy, right in the middle of Brixton, is a rare independent multi-screen venue, which on top of the latest mainstream and offbeat movies is also a buzzy local venue with film festivals, cafe-bar and live music nights.

In summer, various outdoor screenings take place across the capital (unpredictable British weather permitting). Past events have been staged in the city's parks, places such as Somerset House, and Tooting Bec Lido has even held a series of 'dive-in' movies. Check local listings for details.

London Film Festival

The London Film Festival, which celebrated its 50th birthday in 2006, showcases over 300 films from more than 60 countries every October. Rather than aiming to rival Cannes or Venice, the festival prides itself on being accessible to the general public – see www.lff.org.uk.

BFI IMAX Cinema
South Bank

0870 7872525
www.bfi.org.uk

The UK's largest cinema screen (almost the height of five double-decker buses) and wraparound sound combine to deliver the ultimate 3D experience.

Cine Lumiere
South Kensington

7073 1350
www.institut-francais.org.uk

A French-language programme showcasing the best of European and world cinema. Look out for premieres and special screenings introduced by actors and directors.

Clapham Picturehouse
Clapham

0870 7550061
www.picturehouses.co.uk

A vibrant programme of mainstream movies, art house, kids' favourites and classics is shown here. There's a licensed cafe-bar too, with film quiz nights every other Tuesday.

Electric Cinema
Notting Hill

7908 9696
www.electriccinema.co.uk

If you like to watch your movies in comfort, try going Electric. Leather seats and footstools grace this arthouse staple in a trendy Portobello Road location.

Everyman Cinema Club
Hampstead

0870 0664777
www.everymancinema.com

Longstanding classy Hampstead local with bar, bookshop and comfy seats. Sofas for two make this a great place to go for a date.

Gate Picturehouse

Notting Hill

0870 7550063
www.picturehouses.co.uk

Old on the oustside, modern on the inside – snuggle up in this Grade II-listed building with a renovated interior featuring air con, armchairs and double 'love seats'.

ICA Cinematheque

The Mall

7930 3647
www.ica.org.uk

Two screens at the Institute of Contemporary Arts air the more obscure and avant-garde end of cinema, both past and present.

Phoenix Cinema

East Finchley

8883 2233
www.phoenixcinema.co.uk

Thought to be the oldest purpose-built cinema in the UK, the Phoenix is one of London's best-loved locals. Where else can you get a historic art deco interior as well as excellent cake?

Rich Mix

Bethnal Green

7613 7498
www.richmix.org.uk

State-of-the-art screens are hidden away in this former Bethnal Green garment factory, now an excellent cross-cultural arts and media centre.

Riverside Studios

Hammersmith

8237 1111
www.riversidestudios.co.uk

The repertory screen of this west London arts centre on the banks of the Thames is the perfect place to catch a classic on a lazy Sunday afternoon.

Live Music

Shake your head to the sound of electric guitars and pulsating bass lines in the city's mosh-pits, or dress up and nod your head in considered approval to piano recitals at London's concert halls.

A flick through a listings magazine will leave you in no doubt that London's gig scene is as lively as ever. While chart acts and new favourites stop off at the Carling Academies in Islington or Brixton, Koko in Camden, The Forum in Kentish Town or the Shepherd's Bush Empire, the real megastars play Hammersmith Apollo, Earls Court or Wembley Arena.

If you are willing to take pot luck, head to Camden where authentic pub rock venues have bands on nightly for little or no admission charge: Dublin Castle, Enterprise, Barfly and The Fusiller & Firkin all have good reputations, while The Bull and Gate in neighbouring Kentish Town showcases new talent. The punk-scarred Electric Ballroom and the hallowed Roundhouse are among Camden's larger music venues, both dripping with myth and magic.

More centrally, the Mean Fiddler on Charing Cross Road is a mid-sized rock venue, and the same company also owns the nearby Astoria – home to Saturday's long-running G-A-Y club where the likes of Kylie and Madonna have camped it up – and the Borderline, where you'll find alternative country and low-fi. Oxford Street's legendary 100 Club lays claim to being the oldest live music venue in town and ensures its survival with a music policy embracing indie, jazz, blues and DJ nights. Among various Brixton hotspots are the rock-orientated Windmill, and Brixton JAMM for drum & bass and hip-hop.

The beating heart of London's jazz scene in the 1950s, Soho still has a clutch of nightspots – Ronnie Scott's and Pizza Express Jazz Club among them – where the trumpet solo lives on. For classical fans, the South Bank has three excellent concert halls and hosts free foyer recitals. Also on the classical circuit are the Barbican Centre, Wigmore Hall, St John's Smith Square and St Martin-in-the-Fields on Trafalgar Square, plus of course the Royal Albert Hall for the Proms, but for a less formal and more contemporary skew on the genre try Café Bartok on Camden's Chalk Farm Road.

If you're in town during the summer months, the chances are that there will be an open-air gig or festival going on in one of London's parks or open spaces. Blissed-out crowds spend days and long evenings listening to big name acts at all manner of events and one-off concerts. Hyde Park hosts the stadium acts, while dance music festivals and freebies can be enjoyed at Regent's Park, Clapham Common and Finsbury Park.

Street Music

Many up-and-coming musicians try their material on the unforgiving public in the form of busking. A lot of the brave souls on the streets and underpasses of London are incredibly talented, so keep your ears open – today's busker could be tomorrow's superstar in the making.

Bush Hall
Hammersmith

8222 6955
www.bushhallmusic.co.uk

This atmospheric early 20th century dance hall, also formerly a soup kitchen, bingo hall and snooker den, is now restored for intimate gigs and unsigned band nights.

Dingwalls
Camden

7428 0010
www.dingwalls.com

A Camden Lock stalwart that puts on a packed schedule of indie and rock bands, and regularly features up-and-coming underground artists. This venue, all on one level, can cater for about 500 guests.

Jazz Cafe
Camden

0870 0603777
www.jazzcafe.co.uk

Funk, soul, hip-hop and jazz mainstays play at this cool venue. Make a night of it by booking a table on the upstairs gallery and watch the music while you eat.

The Luminaire
Kilburn

7372 7123
www.theluminaire.com

The Luminaire sets new standards of comfort and friendliness for gig-goers on Kilburn High Road. There's a Thai restaurant and a bar downstairs, with the music played upstairs.

Notting Hill Arts Club
Notting Hill

7460 4459
www.nottinghillartsclub.com

Hip club that features regular live music slots and DJ sets from punk veterans and indie celebrities.

Scala

King's Cross

7833 2022
www.scala-london.co.uk

This former cinema in King's Cross plays host to up-and-coming indie acts, plus well-known artists such as Joss Stone and The Scissor Sisters. Regular club nights are also staged.

The Spitz

Spitalfields

7392 9032
www.spitz.co.uk

World music, folk, beats, jazz, blues and electronica are all played in this cosy candlelit space, and there's a bar, bistro and gallery downstairs.

ULU

Bloomsbury

7664 2000
www.ulu.co.uk/ululive

A perennial indie-kid favourite, this student union bar is a popular gig venue, and not just for the cheap booze.

Union Chapel

Islington

7226 1686
www.unionchapel.org.uk

Unique gothic surroundings at this active church on Upper Street create one of London's most inspiring places to enjoy live music. With all profits being used for charitable projects, it's refreshingly uncorporate.

The Vortex Jazz Club

Dalston

7993 3643
www.vortexjazz.co.uk

The backstreets of Dalston are the location for this unique club showcasing new and trad jazz – a night here is a very different experience from the big name West End venues.

Comedy & Cabaret

Variety really is the spice of life as the capital embraces comedy greats old and new, and throws its arms wide open to welcome the burlesque revival.

Comedy

From slapstick and general silliness to controversial and highly political, the UK comedy scene is incredibly diverse – and London showcases more rib-crackingly good, groaningly bad and absurdly ugly acts than anywhere else in the world.

Venues range from shiny specialist sit-down joints, such as the Jongleurs chain (which has clubs in Bow, Battersea and Camden), to smoky pubs and seedy backrooms. Many London clubs give new talent the opportunity to shine or flop, and old hands the chance to try out fresh material. The Comedy Store in Leicester Square has spawned a number of other clubs close by. Established venues known for their good laughs include Lee Hurst's Backyard Comedy Club in east London, Southwark's Menier Chocolate Factory, the Amused Moose nights (various venues) and Downstairs at the King's Head in Crouch End. Elsewhere, Student Union comedy nights are a good bet for a cheap, fun night out with the chance to catch, and heckle, newcomers to the scene.

Cabaret and Burlesque

Casting a knowing wink in the direction of 1920s Berlin and Soho's seedy strip joint heyday, contemporary cabaret

Canal Café Theatre, Little Venice	www.canalcafetheatre.com
Picturesque Little Venice is the setting for this long-running upstairs comedy and fringe theatre venue.	7289 6054

Comedy Café, Shoreditch	www.comedycafe.co.uk
Book a table for an evening's stand-up entertainment at this purpose-built Shoreditch supper club.	7739 5706

Ealing Studios	www.ealingstudios.com
Film studio that produced *The Lavender Hill Mob* is the perfect backdrop to long-running comedy club Ha Bloody Ha.	8567 6655

Red Rose Comedy Club, Finsbury Park	www.redrosecomedy.co.uk
North London club with pub prices, good for catching big-name comics playing warm-up gigs.	0870 0600100

Up The Creek, Greenwich	www.up-the-creek.com
Popular comedy and cabaret club in south-east London, with a restaurant on site.	8858 4581

in the capital is truly alive and high-kicking. Feather boas, suspenders and frilly knickers have gone mainstream as punters dress up as flappers and Chicago gangsters to enjoy ever-so-slightly naughty fun and frolics. The glitzy Soho Revue Bar leads the way with drag acts, big bands, conjurers and goodness knows what else, with events such as PS2 Cabaret Room at Bethnal Green's trendy restaurant-bar Bistrotheque and Sunday afternoon's Late Late Lunch at Farringdon club Turnmills gaining loyal followings. Drag queens are a staple of gay pubs such as Camden's Black Cap and Royal Vauxhall Tavern in south London, while the drag king reigns supreme at Club Wotever.

Theatre

The lights, the buzz of the audience as the curtain goes up, a fiver for a small tub of icecream – theatre remains an irresistible part of the London experience.

West End

London's Theatreland is famous the world over and, with an average of more than 12 million people seeing a play or musical each year and spending some £250 million on tickets, it's a huge moneyspinner for the city's tourist industry. Despite the possibilities offered by a multimedia world, the immediacy and unpredictability of live performance remains hard to beat. Although box office smashes such as *Phantom of the Opera* and *Mary Poppins* and Broadway transfers featuring Hollywood stars tend to be booked up months in advance, it is always possible to get tickets at short notice for long-running favourites and lesser-known gems at the more creaky – but nonetheless charming – West End auditoriums.

Off-West End

While Theatreland is dominated by showstopping musicals, camp thrillers and giddy farces, the Royal National Theatre on the South Bank mounts highbrow classics and cutting-edge new work. The Royal Shakespeare Company is resident at the Barbican, while the Bard's work can also be seen at Shakespeare's Globe, a loving recreation of an Elizabethan theatre in Borough. A destination perfect for a summer's evening is the Open Air Theatre in the heart of Regent's Park. Those with more adventurous tastes may find something of interest at The Old Vic, near Waterloo, where Hollywood's Kevin Spacey presides over an imaginative programme of revivals, and the Royal Court, on Sloane Square, known for its ground-breaking productions. For politically engaged theatre, try Kilburn's Tricycle or the Arcola Theatre in Dalston.

Fringe

All over the capital legions of enthusiastic small theatre troupes put on productions at fringe venues, which are often tiny auditoriums squeezed into pub backrooms or studios attached to larger venues. Islington is a good hunting ground, boasting the Old Red Lion, Hen & Chickens, King's Head and the lovely child-friendly Little Angel theatres. Other fringe venues with notable reputations include the Bush Theatre in Shepherd's Bush, the BAC in Battersea, Oval House in Kennington and Finborough Theatre in Chelsea.

Tickets

Tickets for all shows can be purchased directly from the venue's box office, as well as by phone or online through agencies such as Ticketmaster (which slap on hefty booking fees). If you're looking for a cheap last-minute deal or returns from a sold-out show, your best bet is to head to Leicester Square. Here you'll find several outlets offering cut-price deals on that day's performances, as well as restricted-view seats. The 'tkts' booth is the Society of London Theatre's official discount outlet (there's also one in Canary Wharf).

Ballet, Dance & Opera

If your evening's entertainment is not complete until the fat lady sings (or the muscular man pirouettes), you won't be disappointed in what London has to offer.

Ballet & Dance

The Royal Opera House in Covent Garden is home to the Royal Ballet, and Sadler's Wells in Islington also stages lavish ballet (and contemporary dance) productions in its fabulous modern auditorium. The Queen Elizabeth Hall and Purcell Room on the South Bank both offer a varied programme of dance, and two smaller venues in the West End, The Place Theatre in Bloomsbury and Peacock Theatre in Covent Garden, give space to smaller companies offering everything from jazz dance to children's ballet.

Opera

Covent Garden boasts two top-class opera venues – the Royal Opera House, which was refurbished in the 1990s, and the London Coliseum, home to the English National Opera. The Opera House is the more formal (and pricey) of the two, but both sell a percentage of tickets at low prices (check for availability). At the National Opera you can enjoy classics and modern work performed in English, whereas the ROH's programme is primarily made up of traditional classics. Other auditoriums where arias are regularly sung are Sadler's Wells, Hackney Empire, the Barbican and the Royal Albert Hall.

Opera House (Rob Moore)

Shopping

Buy, Buy, Buy

From upmarket fashion boutiques to cheap and cheerful markets, plus some of the world's best-known department stores, London offers ample opportunity to enjoy filling your shopping bags and shrinking your bank balance.

London is home to more than 40,000 stores, plus the world's longest shopping thoroughfare, Oxford Street, which also contains the world's largest fashion store, Topshop. Specialist outlets selling rare and bespoke items sit alongside hip boutiques, department stores and hundreds of high street shops.

There are many different areas to shop in London, and each comes with its own character. At one end of Oxford Street, which does high street like nowhere else, Tottenham Court Road is cluttered with electronics stores, while nearby Soho is stacked with kitsch, independent shops, with a focus on alternative music. If it's glamour you want, London has it in spades: Bond Street and Knightsbridge's designer stores invite decadent splashing out and wistful window shopping. It's easy to spend a fortune here if you have the desire (and the money), but London is also a fabulous place for hunting down a bargain, provided you know where to look. Shopping malls and high street clothing stores offer good value for money and have frequent sales, second-hand shops are fun for a rummage, while vintage clothing stores and exchanges sell quality discounted designer gear.

The other major suppliers of bargains are markets – almost every major area of London has one of some description. Camden and Portobello Road are two of the biggest, and are a huge draw at weekends – Camden is well known for its alternative fashion and furniture, while Portobello Road specialises in antiques and clothing. Flower fans head for Columbia Road in Bethnal Green on a Sunday, while foodies flock to Borough on Fridays and Saturdays for the finest produce, both local and imported. Bargaining is acceptable at markets, if not welcomed or anticipated, and stallholders tend to be friendlier than your average high-street shop assistant. That's not to say that shopkeepers in London are the pushy sort – they're more likely to let you browse and come to them if you require any assistance than give you the hard sell.

If you're after something particular, you can bet there's a part of London that specialises

Hidden Extras

The price tag you see on goods in shops includes value added tax (VAT), currently set at 17.5%. Items exempt from this include food, books, newspapers, magazines and children's clothes, but on everything else it is incorporated into the cost. For foreign visitors to the UK, some shops offer a VAT back scheme, allowing you to claim back the tax when leaving the country. Check with a shop before making a purchase.

in it, whether it's textiles in Brick Lane or tailors in Piccadilly. Alternatively, if you'd prefer a bit of everything under one roof, look no further than London's world-famous department stores. Selfridges, Harvey Nichols and Harrods are familiar to many foreign visitors, and some of them have a presence in cities across the globe.

The famous Harrods store is still a draw with visitors and moneyed locals alike, and is pretty much a day out. Now more than 100 years old, it is a symbol of London's continually flourishing shopping scene and is home to seven floors, 28 restaurants and some seriously luxurious toilets. The food hall and gift shop are the best bet for most budgets.

Refund & Exchange

Shops must refund faulty goods if you provide proof of purchase (preferably a receipt). If you simply change your mind, or a garment doesn't fit, most companies will offer an exchange or credit note, or occasionally a refund, if the item is in the same condition in which you bought it. You usually have 28 days in which to return goods, but check the policy when you make your purchase.

Further out of town, shopping centres such as Lakeside in West Thurrock and Bluewater in Kent are an option if you're keen to avoid central London's major stumbling block: the traffic (although even these centres can be extremely busy). The limited, expensive parking and the weekday congestion charge in town make driving there to shop more hassle than it's worth – your best bet is to get up early, put on your comfy shoes, hop on the bus or tube and enjoy a good wander round.

ncy that of london

Lulu's Tou

Shopping Hotspots

Shopping in London is a much-loved national pastime and with the city's fabulous mix of high streets, designer boutiques and urban markets, over-spending is inevitable.

Angel

This varied shopping spot in Islington is easily accessible from central London and is popular with 20 and 30 somethings who've got cash to splash. The main thoroughfare is Upper Street, which runs north towards Highbury from Angel tube. Here, high-street stores mix with boutiques, flower shops, cool bars, restaurants and record shops. There are some fine interior and design boutiques – Aria, Atelier Abigail Ahern and Oliver Bonas are three of the most sought after. SpaceNK caters to all your apothecary needs, the N1 centre offers popular chain stores, while just off Upper Street is Camden Passage, which features a cluster of antique shops.

Bond Street

If one thing characterises the Bond Street area, it's wealth. Split into two halves, New Bond Street and Old Bond Street, both halves are lined with expensive designer stores such as Prada, Louis Vuitton, Armani, Versace and Ralph Lauren, and are populated by designer-clad jet-setters and celebrities. Understated old-school glamour is the favoured look, although famous jewellery shops such as Tiffany, Cartier,

Asprey and Gerrard attract a wider variety of window shoppers. For less expensive fashion, head to South Molton Street, which is good for shoes, and also hosts youthful designer store Browns. On-street parking is limited, but then again most regulars have chauffeurs.

Camden

A London institution, Camden is abuzz with tourists, teens, goths, tramps and everything in between. This is where middle-class shoppers rub shoulders with shady-looking characters as they browse for bargains in Camden High Street's many clothes stores. Shoes are a speciality, and are often cheaper here than elsewhere in town. Edgy, alternative styles, including punk, goth and fetish, are well catered to. Perhaps because of the colourful locals, charity shops such as Mind have interesting stock, while the market provides a hugely popular extension of Camden's range (see p.133). If you want to fill your shopping bag with something alternative, this is the place to come.

Canary Wharf

Aimed at the high-flying professionals who work and live in the area, the shopping centre in the regenerated Canary Wharf is a one-stop-shop for clothing, stationery, food, music, eyewear and more. High-street stores such as Karen Millen, Monsoon and Reiss are all featured here, as is the flagship branch of supermarket Waitrose. This is not the place to come for unique boutiques, although you will find some high-end retailers such as Bang & Olufsen and Mont Blanc.

Covent Garden

Originally best known for its market (which relocated south of the river in the 70s), Covent Garden is now a haven for clothes shoppers with many designer boutiques and high-street stores. Mexx, French Connection, Paul Smith and Ted Baker are all within easy walking distance of each other. Neal's Yard, a delightful little pedestrianised area with health-food shops, street boutiques and restaurants serving in the courtyard, is an oasis from surrounding crowded shopping streets. Neal Street itself is top-notch for trainers, with well-stocked shoe stores such as Offspring and Foot Locker. Nearby Seven Dials offers fashion from Fred Perry, Boxfresh, and Stussy.

High Street Kensington

High Street Ken, as locals call it, packs in the department stores and high-street shops in a slightly less overwhelming fashion than Oxford Street. In Barkers Arcade, the accent is on exclusive designer gear, while chains such as River Island and Miss Selfridge dominate the main street. There's a proliferation of shoe shops and mobile phone stores on the north side. Kensington Church Street mixes high-end boutiques and antiques with bargain clothes shops and a branch of posh eatery Patisserie Valerie. There are plenty of so-so places to wet your whistle, but none beats Babylon in the spectacular surroundings of The Roof Gardens.

Knightsbridge

One of London's poshest retail areas, Knightsbridge attracts wealthy shoppers and day trippers keen to experience famous department store Harrods. This vast shop is worth a visit for its specialist fashion floors and spectacular food hall, plus oddities such as its pampered pet store. Smaller rival Harvey Nichols boasts three floors of designer gear and a popular bar. Head for Sloane Street for more upmarket fashion names, and to Hans Road for Rigby & Peller, an old-fashioned lingerie boutique that specialises in made-to-measure items. Parking is not cheap here.

Marylebone High Street

An upmarket but accessible alternative to nearby Oxford Street, Marylebone is a good bet for specialist shops. Highlights include La Fromagerie cheese shop and Ginger Pig organic butchers (both on Moxon Street, just off the main thoroughfare), and independent bookshop Daunts, which has a good range of travel and cookery volumes. The Conran Shop is a stylish place to browse for gifts and furniture, and the high street's charity shops are a cut above the rest – although unfortunately they know the worth of their designer clothes and price accordingly. There's no shortage of gastro pubs and restaurants in the area to fuel your shopping spree.

Notting Hill

There's a fashionable-but-edgy vibe to Notting Hill, which takes in both swanky upmarket residences and run-down council housing. As a result, it's popular with affluent trendies and kids looking for street style. The area is known for its varying styles, from pricey fashion boutiques such as The

Dispensary, antiques shops on Portobello Road and music stores such as the second-hand Music and Video Exchange on Pembridge Road. Excellent florist Wild at Heart and boutique jeweller EcOne can be found further towards Westbourne Grove, where many shoppers seek out fashionable bars, pubs and restaurants, and the Electric Cinema, which has a funky design and comfy sofas.

Oxford Street

London's busiest shopping street draws tourists and locals in their droves seeking big-name brands and, increasingly, bargains. Many fashion stores have sales every few weeks, and with chains such as Zara, Mango, Marks & Spencer, New Look and H&M, comparison shopping is easy to do in an afternoon (if you can handle the crowds). Between Bond Street and Marble Arch tube stations, department stores dominate, including John Lewis, House of Fraser and Selfridges, while Regent Street offers more high street fashion, designer stores and the famous Hamleys toy shop. Oxford Street is also worth a look for lingerie shops, huge Virgin, HMV and Borders stores, and cheap temporary shops selling warehouse leftovers. Just be prepared to deal with the crowds, especially on weekends.

Museums, Not Malls

Museum and gallery shops offer a great array of books, knick-knacks, souvenirs and gift ideas. Be sure to pop into the store of whatever gallery or museum you visit – you're guaranteed to find something interesting, and may even pick up a post-exhibition bargain.

Bursting at the seams with character, shoppers and bargains, spending a morning or afternoon in one of London's many colourful markets is a great way to shop, as well as a fascinating cultural experience.

Berwick Street Market
Soho, W1

If you're after a traditional London market experience in the centre of town, head to Soho's Berwick Street for the all-day market, open daily except Sundays. Fruit and veg sellers have all the cockney patter you could want, and the apples and pears are reliably fresh. It's a good spot to pick up fish too, and there's an array of cheap goods such as CDs and accessories. The local market traders' pub was transformed into a trendy gastropub, The Endurance, a few years ago, but this and other watering holes nearby still attract a lively mix of stallholders and media types. ⊖ Piccadilly Circus

Borough Market
Borough, SE1

Borough has become massively popular in recent years thanks to its specialist stalls selling fresh, often organic, food and drink. Fine wines, ports and ciders are readily available, and you'll find meats such as game and even ostrich. Stop off for a cider or

sample some cheese before grabbing your lunch at Brindisa, which has eager punters queuing up for their grilled chorizo sandwiches. There's imported produce as well as home-grown, and while prices aren't on the cheap side, the quality is typically excellent. The buzzing pubs around the edge of the market also add to the weekend atmosphere. The market is open Thursdays, Fridays and Saturdays until 16:00. ⊖ London Bridge

Brick Lane Market
Bethnal Green, E1

While Brick Lane's street market errs on the cheap and cheerful – selling second-hand clothing and furniture – the 'Sunday UpMarket' in the Old Truman Brewery, Ely's Yard, is another story. Stylish homeware, jewellery, fashions and hand-made accessories are the pick, with music stalls and plenty of international food. The punters reflect Brick Lane's increasingly hip image, making the area almost as famous for its fashion as its curry houses. There are many textile stores here too, and look out for signs for temporary designer clothing sales in the surrounding streets. ⊖ Shoreditch

Broadway Market
Hackney, E8

A relatively small set-up full of character, Broadway mixes a farmers' market with stalls selling trendy clothes and accessories. It's a lovely spot to browse for that must-have handbag, cushion or hat before picking up some unusual cheese, meat, mushrooms or even a cake for dinner. You can usually try before you buy – quite useful given that the range can be almost overwhelming. There are a few flower stalls with colourful bunches. Pop into the Dove pub to sample its wild-boar burgers and extensive Belgian beer list. The market is open on Saturdays from 09:00 to 17:00. ⊖ Bethnal Green

Camden Market
Camden, NW1

Vibrant Camden is actually a collection of smaller, individual markets based around Camden High Street, with a mixture of street stalls and permanent buildings. Camden Stables Market is one of the most popular, selling vintage clothing, alternative fashion, antiques, furniture and quirky crafts, as well as international takeaway food. Camden Lock specialises in hand-crafted products, while Canal Market, overlooking Regent's Canal, offers accessories, music, jewellery and collectables. Buck Street Market is popular with teens for T-shirts and jewellery, as is the indoor Electric Ballroom on Camden High Street and the former fruit and veg market on Inverness Street. Weekends are busiest, although many stalls open seven days a week. ⊖ Camden Town

Columbia Road Flower Market
Bethnal Green, E2

This is a cheerful and colourful place to spend (an early) Sunday morning. Crammed into one long street, the market has a dedicated customer base who travel from across London, and beyond, every weekend. It is the best place in town to pick up a relatively cheap, fresh bunch of flowers. Traders are friendly and may well cut you a deal, particularly at lunchtime when

the market is starting to wind down – although early-bird deals are possible too, when the range is more extensive. Prices are competitive and products varied: you can find all manner of exotic and rare plants and shrubs. ⊖ Bethnal Green

Old Spitalfields Market
The City, E1

Spitalfields has become a fashionable, friendly alternative to Camden Market, albeit considerably smaller. Its stalls are housed under one large roof and offer original designs in the fields of interiors, fashion, arts and craft, as well as food – its original product in the 1600s. A selection of stalls is open all week, except for Saturdays: deli on Wednesdays, antiques on Thursdays, fashion and art on Fridays. But it's Sundays, with a bohemian mix of gifts, quirky clothing and vintage gear on offer, that are most popular. ⊖ Liverpool Street

Portobello Road Market
Westbourne Grove, W10

Antiques dominate the south end of this long, fashionable west London street that hosts market stalls every Saturday, both on the road and in its arcades. Rare vintage costumes, militaria, brass, books, jewellery and paintings can all be found here. Food stalls are most prevalent further down the street, followed by clothing and jewellery in a wide range of styles and price ranges. Funky fashions typify the Portobello Green arcade, and many more hip designers do brisk business under the large canopy nearby. ⊖ Notting Hill Gate

Department Stores

London's major department stores are so well-known that they top many visitors' must-see lists, while others are just great places to shop.

Fortnum & Mason

181 Regent St, W1   7734 8040

This gentrified store, which historically has had royal approval, was founded by one of Queen Anne's entrepreneurial footmen in 1707. He started his business by selling spare royal candle wax, and by the 1800s it was established as London's major supplier of exotic and fine foods. Today it is still a specialist in caviar, cheese, chocolate, teas and coffees from around the world, as well as wine, spirits and hampers. There's a quirky department devoted to food oddities with interesting histories such as Pusser's Dark Navy Marmalade, created to commemorate Nelson's victory over the French at Trafalgar. ⊖ Piccadilly Circus

Harrods

87-135 Brompton Rd, SW1   7730 1234

Famously opulent Harrods came from surprisingly humble beginnings – it started life as a wholesale grocer in London's East End in 1834. In 1849 it moved to larger premises in Knightsbridge (where it has since stayed) and broadened its remit considerably. Now almost anything is sold over its seven floors (Noel Coward once bought an alligator from here), and

the store is worth a visit, regardless of whether you're buying. Departments include fashion, food and drink, children's clothes and toys, sports equipment, home furnishings and even a pet shop. There are 28 restaurants, including Planet Harrods and Mo's Diner, and afternoon tea at The Georgian Restaurant is a decadent must-do. The Harrods gift shop has some surprisngly affordable items, and the signature teddy bear always makes a great souvenir. ⊖ Knightsbridge

Harvey Nichols
109-125 Knightsbridge, SW1   7235 5000

Born of a Sloane Square linen shop in 1813, Harvey Nichols is now the toast of the privileged classes and continues to expand across the UK and internationally. Customers' wallets are regularly emptied in men and women's fashion and accessory departments, the foodhall, a furniture emporium and a beauty hall. The store is proud of its exclusive image (it stocks many limited-edition ranges) and is aimed at a wealthier crowd: Anya Hindmarch Pablo Logo travelbags sell for £345, Chanel limited edition compacts from £22 and Culti sofas for around £4,700. The famous Fifth Floor hosts a restaurant, cafe and bar, frequented by London's 'ladies who lunch'. ⊖ Knightsbridge

House Of Fraser
318 Oxford St, W1   0870 1607268

House of Fraser is one of the UK's biggest department store chains, and the same company also owns and trades as Army & Navy, Binns, Dickins & Jones, Dingles, and Rackhams.

The store is hot on fashion, make-up and homeware, and also stocks big-name electrical goods, accessories and food. There are several branches of House of Fraser in London, and several have mother and baby rooms for changing and feeding. Other facilities include a free courier service within the Square Mile (City store only), complimentary personal shoppers and an alterations service. The Oxford Street and Victoria branches both have restaurants. ⊖ Oxford Circus

John Lewis
278-306 Oxford St, W1   7629 7711

John Lewis opened his first store on Oxford Street in 1864, and in 1905 bought his second store, Peter Jones, in Sloane Square. There are now 26 John Lewis department stores across the UK, and the company is also the parent of high-class supermarket chain Waitrose. The company's philosophy is that the happiness of its staff (which it calls partners), rather than its customers, is its ultimate purpose, reasoning that happy workers make for happy shoppers. The range of goods helps satisfy spenders too – departments include audio and TV, computing, electrical, fashion, beauty, home and garden, nursery, sports and toys, plus a cafe. ⊖ Bond Street

Liberty
210-220 Regent St, W1   7734 1234

Perhaps the most aesthetically pleasing of all London's department stores, Liberty opened in 1875 selling ornaments, fabric and objects of art from the Orient. The store used to occupy a house on Regent Street, now it occupies two properties with an adjoining walkway. The idea was to bring beautiful things to ordinary people, and fine goods were sourced from Java, Persia and India. Today the store offers gorgeous stationery, accessories, homewares, and clothing, although prices are perhaps no longer so accessible to 'ordinary people'. There is also a Liberty concession in Terminal 3 of Heathrow Airport. ✛ Oxford Circus

Selfridges

400 Oxford St, W1   0870 8377377

Selfridges has been around since 1909, and has been credited with putting Oxford Street on the world retail map. It sells high-street and designer fashion, and there's an excellent cosmetics floor, as well as homeware, electrical goods and gourmet food. A visit isn't just about shopping though – you can have your nails done, get your bike repaired, your ears pierced or book a trip to the theatre. Look out for the window displays at Christmas and regular themed events, when the store often hosts live music and looks more like a modern art gallery.

✛ Bond Street

A Night On The Shops

Forget bars and clubs – department stores are the new place to socialise. In some stores the food and drink is as much an attraction as the shopping; Harvey Nichols draws more people to its Fifth Floor restaurant and bar than to its soap and candle section, Harrods has a staggering 28 restaurants, and Selfridges operates five cafes, four restaurants, three bars and several snack bars.

Best of London

For books go to…

Foyles

113-119 Charing Cross Rd, WC2   7437 5660

Foyles is probably London's most famous book store, supplying generations of readers since it opened in 1906. The building is huge, and the selection almost overwhelming; text books of all kinds can be found here, as can general fiction and specialist genres, plus an impressive collection of printed music. The ordering service is excellent, and Foyles vows to supply any book in print. There's also a jazz shop and cafe on the first floor. ⊖ Tottenham Court Road

For clothes go to…

Topshop

216 Oxford St, W1   0845 1214519

Massively popular, and literally massive, this women's clothing store has a huge range of fashionable threads – a veritable heaven for the fashion weary and the style wired. There are many concessions here including Faith shoes and Calvin Klein underwear, and the quality is excellent, especially considering the prices (around £30 to £40 for a pair of jeans). There's a decent vintage section too, although this steers more towards the pricey side for the high street. If you're not sure what suits you, Topshop offers a style-advice service, and if it all gets too much, you can take a break in the cafe. Kate Moss has now leant her fashionista skills to Topshop and the crowds will no doubt follow. ⊖ Oxford Circus

For classy furniture go to…

Heal's

234 King's Rd, SW3　　　　　　　　　　7636 1666

An established London store with branches in Tottenham Court Road and King's Road, Heal's is a high-end furniture and home accessories outlet with great designs in sofas, tables and lighting. The shops have a great gifts section and sell stylish coffee table books, cool kitchenware and designer bath accessories. Most items are exclusive to Heal's, and it also offers a bespoke sofa-design service – you can pick your fabric and style, although most designs would look best in a large, spacious home (something most of its well-heeled customers probably possess). ⊖ Sloane Square

For musical instruments go to…

Chappell

152-160 Wardour St, W1　　　　　　　　7432 4400

Chappell has been around since 1811 (Charles Dickens was reputedly a fan) and is widely considered to be the most comprehensive music shop in London. It has a huge range of instruments, as well as a large printed music section. Pianos, brass and woodwind instruments are popular purchases, as are a few things that weren't around in Dickensian times, such as mics, amps and mixers. Plug-in equipment such as electric violins is usually rigged up and connected to headphones so you can have a play. Even if you're not musical, hanging out in Chappell is cool. ⊖ Oxford Circus

For chic stationery go to…

Smythson

40 New Bond St, W1   7629 8558

One of London's most famous, and expensive, stationers, Smythson supplies royals and rich folk who delight in its high quality and stylish designs. You can have your envelopes and paper personalised here, or you can choose from the Smythson watermarked ready-to-write range. You'll also find photo albums and frames, leather handbags and jewellery boxes, special occasion cards, diaries and leather desk and office accessories. ⊖ Bond Street

For kids go to…

Hamleys

188-196 Regent St, W1   0870 3332455

If you're looking for toys in London, there's only one place to go: Hamleys. Its Regent Street store has seven busy floors of toys, gadgets and games for all ages. There's an enormous range of products, including an own-brand line of toys. Staff dotted around the store demonstrate toys such as bubble-blowing machines and remote-controlled cars to fascinated kids, and each floor is dedicated to specific lines or ranges. As well as modern gadgets, Hamleys also stocks old favourites such as Fuzzy Felt, Scalextric and Play-Doh. Be prepared to spend at least a couple of hours here – whether or not you have children in tow. The good news is there's a cafe on the top floor. ⊖ Oxford Circus

For luxury food go to…

Harrods
87-135 Brompton Rd, SW1   7730 1234

This famed food hall is home to some of the world's most mouthwatering (and exclusive) goodies. The opulent displays of gourmet chocolates, luxurious Laduree macaroons and deli dishes attract spectators as well as shoppers; Easter and Christmas are a treat for both the eyes and the taste-buds. There are also some fun Harrods souvenirs and the regular wine tastings might convince you that spending a small fortune on a box of biscuits is a good idea! ⊖ Knightsbridge

For souvenirs go to…

Fancy That of London
3-4 Station Approach, Marylebone Rd, NW1   7925 2647

You'll find souvenir shops all over the city, with everything from Union Jack tea towels to mini London buses vying for your attention. Central shopping and entertainment locations such as Piccadilly Circus, Covent Garden and Oxford Street are all particularly well served, as are areas with museums like South Kensington and attractions such as the Tower of London and Buckingham Palace. Fancy That of London has three shops, with its Baker Street Emporium worth a mention for its 19th century, Sherlock Holmes style decor and theatre ticket concessions. There's also a good choice of cheaper items so there's no excuse for neglecting the folks back home.

⊖ Knightsbridge

Going Out

Food & Drink

London boasts one of the most vibrant and diverse social scenes in the world, where people come together to have a great time. From cosy pubs to beautiful bars and exclusive restaurants, there are venues for all tastes and budgets.

Different areas have their own distinct vibes and faithful followings. For an eclectic blend of trendy and trashy, Soho still delivers. Or, join the retro-funk artists and creative types in lounge bars and banging clubs in the 'new cool' Hoxton and Shoreditch. Fulham and King's Road are good enough for young royalty and offer choices from cheery pop to dark dance, but some bars can be a bit pretentious. Mayfair is still the setting for designer-clad beautiful people slinking between the VIP lounges of private members' clubs.

Upper Street in Islington offers the highest concentration of restaurants and bars; forget the chains and discover more than 100 venues packed on to one strip. In the back alleys around Oxford Street, hidden bars come alive after dusk offering jazz and live music. But the heart of the capital's music scene lies to the north in Camden, where you can see anything from dirty old blues to funky new tunes.

Like many capital cities, social hours are dictated by office hours; there's a weeknight rush from 18:00 to 23:00, but at the weekends things tend to get going from 21:00 and last well into the early hours.

Soho

Soho has witnessed scenes of debauchery for centuries. It has swung from trendy to sleazy and back again, and now has firmly established itself as the city's best bet for food, drink and frolics.

Busaba Eathai
Thai
106-110 Wardour St, W1
7258 6863

Every night of the week fans of fabulous Thai cuisine queue under the awnings of this restaurant run by Alan Yau. Tables are communal and often cramped but that doesn't detract from simple, well-priced dishes from the grill, wok or curry pot. A no-reservations policy requires early arrival, but turnover is fast and the food is worth waiting for. ⊖ Oxford Circus

Floridita
Latin American
100 Wardour St, W1
7314 4000

While dancers swing to the in-house band, chefs sweat to deliver delicious chargrilled lobster and spit-roast pig. The staff are as proficient on the dancefloor as they are at serving, but don't be persuaded to leave your table without sampling the desserts (you can work the excess off later). ⊖ Oxford Circus

Gama
Japanese
139 Wardour St, W1
0871 0751189

Gama is one of the few spots in Chinatown that is mainly frequented by young Japanese and Korean diners, which suggests their chow is authentic. The bulgogi, a Korean-style barbecue, is delicious. It's a relaxed canteen-style diner and is great value, with late night cocktails and salsa music downstairs at J's Lounge. ⊖ Oxford Circus

Hakkasan
8 Hanway Place, W1

Chinese
7907 1888

This Michelin-starred Chinese restaurant is one of the best fine-dining options in the capital. The decor is stunning and the cuisine is deserving of its reputation. Your tastebuds will be in heaven but your wallet might hurt for a while. For a lighter (and cheaper) taste of Hakkasan, dim sum and cocktails are served in the lively bar area. ⊖ Oxford Circus

Imli
167-169 Wardour St, W1

Indian
7287 4243

It's not uncommon in an Indian restaurant to order a few dishes to share, but Imli takes this one step further by offering 'modern Indian tapas'. This is not just a new gimmick but culinary wizardry. A choice of dozens of innovative dishes, brought to the table as and when they are ready, give you and your fellow diners the freedom to sample Indian cuisine with an original twist. ⊖ Tottenham Court Road

St. Moritz
161 Wardour St, W1

European
7734 3324

Fondues haven't been a staple of the dinner party scene since the late 1980s but the original Swiss dish served in this rustic restaurant is worth revisiting. There are five traditional cheese options, an oil fondue for dipping meat and a fondue chinois, a stock hotpot that quickly braises fine slices of beef.

⊖ Oxford Circus

Ooze
Italian
62 Goodge St, W1
7436 9444

A 'risotto bar' is a refreshingly new concept for a dish as old as Italy itself, and Ooze pulls off this twist without appearing tacky or trendy. Purists have their choice of homely classics, but those who want to challenge their taste buds will not be disappointed by the chef's innovative creations. Low salt, low fat and low carb choices are marked, and the cheery atmosphere will brighten any gloomy London day. ⊖ Goodge Street

Freedom
Bar
60-66 Wardour St, W1
0871 3325262

Freedom is a flamboyant and fabulous bar that hosts art exhibitions, film premieres and glamorous after-show parties. Upstairs the stylish and wildly colourful cocktail bar is popular for leisurely daytime drinking with a few tasty snacks on the side, and the atmosphere gets livelier as the evening draws in. Dancing is the name of the game in the large basement club, with poles for people to work their magic on. An open-house policy welcomes gay and straight people. ⊖ Piccadilly Circus

The Ship
Pub
116 Wardour St, W1
7437 8446

This massively popular old English style pub is crammed every night of the week. There's great music chosen by the landlords and the noise level rises as the evening goes on. If you're looking for a quieter time to gather your thoughts, or to pen a song like The Clash did under the staircase here, visit on a midweek lunchtime. ⊖ Oxford Circus

Lucky Voice
52 Poland St, W1

Karaoke Bar
7439 3660

Probably the coolest venue in town to sing your heart out in, this hip bar also serves top-notch cocktails and sushi. The nine rooms fit up to 12 crooners and all have touchscreen monitors and 5,000 songs to choose from. It's advisable to book ahead. Prices start from £20 per hour per room for four people (£60 an hour for eight people on weekends).
⊖ Oxford Circus

Ronnie Scott's Jazz Club
47 Frith St, W1

Nightclub
7439 0747

Generations of music lovers have visited the legendary Ronnie Scott's. Some of the true greats have performed here; today's talent is still outstanding and the atmosphere euphoric. Come to dine on the fine food or just sit with a drink in the tiered seats overlooking the stage – you'll be entertained all evening. Open until 03:00. ⊖ Tottenham Court Rd

The Admiral Duncan
54 Old Compton St, W1

Gay & Lesbian
7437 5300

The Admiral Duncan has risen triumphantly after a nail bomb attack in 1999 to become a symbol against prejudice. It's now one of the most visited gay pubs in Soho and has a vibrant

Floridita

atmosphere. There is a small dancefloor, the decor is fresh and bright and the music is good. ⊖ Leicester Square

Candy Bar

Gay & Lesbian

4 Carlisle St, W1   7494 4041

The ground floor is good for post-work drinks and the lounge upstairs offers a more relaxed vibe. After some delicious cocktails, go down to the bijou club, where DJs, live acts and karaoke are there to entertain. This was the first London club to have licensed lesbian pole dancing and gay men are welcome as guests. ⊖ Tottenham Court Road

G-A-Y

Gay & Lesbian

Astoria, 157 Charing Cross Road, W1   7434 0403

As London's largest gay venue this offers a range of fun and flashy nights out. The regular house nights on Thursdays are eternally popular, and big-name performers like Kylie Minogue have played G-A-Y's Saturday Big Night Out. Fridays see 'Camp Attack' with cheesy tunes, while Mondays host the Pink Pounder when entry is just a pound. ⊖ Tottenham Court Road

Soho Revue Bar

Gay & Lesbian

11 Walkers Court, W1   7439 4089

This glamorous, kitcsch venue is a Soho stalwart. The decadent interior provides a sexy backdrop for drag queens, musicians, DJs and hot dancers. Cocktails are as tasty as the punters who pour through the doors. The Revue Bar is an experience that captures quintessential Soho; sex, entertainment and unadulterated fun. ⊖ Tottenham Court Road

Covent Garden & Leicester S

is London's tourist town, and the first
op for many visitors on a night out. It is
right and buzzing, and beyond the ticket
vendors, luke-warm burgers and union
flag knickers are some hidden food and
drink gems.

Calabash

African

Africa Centre, 38 King St, WC2   7836 1976

This small restaurant in the basement of the Africa Centre
lets diners explore the continent's many wonderful cuisines.
Traditional ingredients are used, like cassava flour, teff and
the increasingly familiar okra, yam and plantain. The stews are
rich and filling and there are Kenyan and South African beers
available to help wash it all down. The setting is plain, but
drummers occasionally start up with vibrant African
rhythms to help breathe new life into the room.

⊖ Covent Garden

The Ivy

European

1 West St, WC2   7836 4751

This celebrated haunt has been entertaining London society
since 1917. The decor of dark wood and white linen is simple
and elegant, and lifted by the hubbub of conversation and
laughter. The waiting list is long but when your time comes it
feels special. Pre-theatre and weekend set lunch menus make
it accessible to those on a tighter budget. ⊖ Leicester Square

Canela
Latin American

33 Earlham St, WC2 · 7240 6926

Despite its stripped cafe decor, Canela should not be overlooked for an informal evening meal. There is also a welcome array of wheat and gluten-free cakes and breads to go with healthy fresh ginger or herb infusions, or, if you prefer, indulgent vegetarian dishes such as lasagne oozing cheese and rich tomato sauce. ⊖ Covent Garden

Ed's Easy Diner
American

12 Moor St, W1 · 7434 4439

Ed's is a 1950s-style American diner in all its glory. Black-and-white chequered tiles and red leather stools with mini jukeboxes on every table make it a fun place to stop while out in the West End. Stacks of pancakes come with slivers of crunchy bacon and maple syrup, while thick malted milkshakes are made in traditional flavours as well as greedy butterscotch, coffee and banana, or peanut butter. ⊖ Leicester Square

K-Box
Karaoke Bar

7-9 Cranbourn St, WC2 · 7287 8868

It may not be the swankiest, but it's probably London's biggest 'pure' karaoke venue. Like Lucky Voice (7439 3660), the rooms are fitted with touchscreen karaoke systems, there's Asian food on the menu, and a bar. A room holding eight people costs from £35 to £60 per hour, depending on the time and day. K-Box is open from 18:00 until 03:00 Thursday to Saturday and 18:00 until 23:00 during the rest of the week. ⊖ Leicester Square

Lowlander Grand Café
Pub

36 Drury Lane, WC2
7379 7446

Look through the door of this beer cafe any night of the week and it will be buzzing, as City types and students come for the 100 Belgian and Dutch beers. Waiter service means you won't have to fight the crowds to get to the bar and the menu descriptions help those who don't know their Dupont from Duimpje. ⊖ Covent Garden

The Opera Rooms at The Chandos
Pub

29 St Martin's Lane, WC2
7836 1401

Leicester Square is teaming with tourists and bright bars, so it's refreshing to see the traditional Opera Rooms still thriving. There are large sofas and low tables in the main bar area, perfect for groups of people to spread out and relax. Food is available from 09:00 until 20:30, from breakfast right through to pies, baguettes and other pub fare.

⊖ Leicester Square

Princess Louise
Pub

208 High Holborn, WC2
7405 8816

A place of unexpected beauty lies behind the thick wooden doors here. On the walls are gilt mirrors, detailed stained glasswork and intricate plasterwork by master craftsmen of the late 1800s. Even the toilets are 'listed', allegedly. The clientele is a mix of young creatives, suited gents and older regulars, all in the Princess to enjoy relatively cheap drinks and pies, ploughman's platters and pork scratchings.

⊖ Holborn

Westminster, Strand & Piccadilly

The old heart of establishment London, these areas have some charming examples of the city's old grandeur and newer spots catering to out-of-towners and office types on big nights out.

Inn the Park

St James's Park, SW1

British
7451 9999

This beautiful, natural restaurant is as suitable for lunch with the kids as for a three-course business dinner. The wooden structure lies low on the horizon, overlooking 'Duck Island' and the lake. During the day it is bustling as breakfasts and sandwiches are served, and the high-class British dishes come with old-fashioned cutlery and embossed glasses. At night the cocktails add even more sophistication. ⊖ St. James's Park

The Savoy Grill

The Strand, WC2

British
7592 1600

Here you'll find outstanding cuisine, impeccable service and an imposing art deco-styled dining room. Chef Marcus Wareing has prepared dessert for the Queen, so you know you're in good company. During the week it's all networking businessmen and knackered shoppers. Evenings are more elegant, with theatre-goers and romancing couples sliding together in the booths that edge the room. There is no pomp, but just enough ceremony to make you feel special.

⊖ Charing Cross

New Piccadilly Café

Cafe

8 Denman St, W1

7437 8530

This much-loved Italian-owned cafe is (just) keeping the multi-national latte-mongers at bay. The charming proprietor, Lorenzo Marioni, serves cheap, delicious British favourites or big plates of spaghetti to an ageing band of customers and a few new fans. Postcards from grateful guests line the back of the counter as thanks for years of great service. Time stands still here, but the place remains in demand. ⊖ Piccadilly Circus

Below Zero and Absolut Ice Bar London

Bar

29-33 Heddon St, W1

7478 8910

Come here to drink in a freezer. Kept at five degrees below zero you can't stay for long before you begin to lose the feeling in your feet – and that's without accounting for the vodka. The fee for your 40 minute slot includes a goofy thermal poncho and gloves to handle your ice glass. You may feel a spectacle, but everyone else looks the same. Drinks are expensive (a refill will cost £6,) but this is an experience that can't be replicated anywhere else in the country. ⊖ Piccadilly Circus

Heaven

Gay & Lesbian

The Arches, Villiers Street, WC2

7930 2020

Billed as the most famous gay club in London, Heaven is not for the faint hearted. The music goes through your bones and the dancing doesn't stop all week. Nights such as Extreme Euphoria, Fruit Machine and its infamous party night Heaven Saturday have tempted punters for over 25 years. The bars (all seven of them) stay open until 06:00. ⊖ Charing Cross

In the shadow of London's banking monoliths, you can find all manner of fashionable dives and lairy late night shenanigans.

Gaucho Grill

Latin American

1 Bell Inn Yard, EC3

7626 5180

An unassuming entrance takes you down into the old vaults of the Bank of England, which have been converted with dark wood and cow-hide stools into a modern, clean-cut restaurant. The main draw is the Argentinian beef, but the private dining service, excellent cocktails and fine wine collection are ideal if you're celebrating a special occasion. ⊖ **DLR** Bank

Great Eastern Dining Room

Far Eastern

54-56 Great Eastern St, EC2

7613 4545

There are a few modern twists that make this pan-Asian menu stand out from the fusion crowd, but this restaurant really comes alive at night. The decor is dark and music loud so while not the spot for a quiet meal, you can enjoy drinking cocktails in the upstairs bar or dancing until the early hours in the strictly dress-down club beneath. ⊖ ⇄ Old Street

Potemkin Russian Restaurant and Vodka Bar

Russian

144 Clerkenwell Rd, EC1

7278 6661

Cobalt blue walls combined with burgundy and gilt mirrors add a touch of traditional glamour to this modern space. Staff are sweet and helpful at explaining the intricacies of the

Slavic dishes. Begin with a starter accompanied by one of 130 vodkas. Three courses with vodka and bread costs around £20; great value given the size of the portions. ⊖ ⇄ Farringdon

Shish
Arabic/Lebanese
313-319 Old St, EC1
7749 0990

The bright and colourful setting here attracts a funky young crowd, hungry for the signature grilled kebabs. Delicious mezze is perfect for sharing as a starter, followed by shish including marinated lamb, chicken or halloumi cheese, all reasonably priced. This is a fun place to start the evening with a bite to eat and a few cocktails. ⊖ ⇄ Old Street

The Coach and Horses
Pub
26-28 Ray St, EC1
7278 8990

At a time when other pubs are stripping faster than a Soho dancer, the Victorian interior to this beautiful boozer remains delightfully unchanged. There is a good range of beers and ales, and the management has created a fun atmosphere and coupled it with seriously tasty menus. There's a small patio under bright orange awnings at the back, which is a haven for workers in the summer. ⊖ ⇄ Farringdon

The Foundry
Bar
84-86 Great Eastern St, EC2
7739 6900

Walk in to this former bank and you're surrounded by paintings and images, including your own face on a TV screen, snapped by CCTV cameras as you enter (for entertainment rather than security). Poetry readings and art and sound installations attract very artistic folk, so if you want a bar that sums up the bohemian side of the area, this is the place. ⊖ ⇄ Old Street

Home
101–106 Leonard St, EC2
Bar
7684 8618

Decked out in slouch-inducing armchairs, the description 'lounge bar' is utterly appropriate here – you'll soon feel like you've moved in. The three open-plan rooms offer plenty of space for groups, but seem just as appropriate for a romantic date. The tempo picks up between Thursdays and Saturdays, with DJs mixing their beats as smoothly as the bartenders do their cocktails. ⊖ ⇄ Old Street

Light Bar
233 Shoreditch High St, E1
Bar
7247 8989

The Light Bar is a bar, restaurant and club so it's easy to spend the whole evening here enjoying the range of bottled beer and cocktails. Outside in the summer the chunky wooden tables, benches and chairs are packed. To keep everyone fuelled there are salads, wraps, burgers and deli platters for sharing and a traditional Sunday lunch. ⊖ ⇄ Liverpool Street

Cargo
Kingsland Viaduct, 83 Rivington St, EC2
Nightclub
7749 7844

A converted railway arch plays host to some of the best new dance music in town. The atmosphere is electric, the people friendly and drinks reasonable. The nibbles are good and the small cafe keeps clubbers going until dawn. ⊖ ⇄ Old Street

Electrowerkz

Nightclub

7 Torrens St, EC1   7837 6419

Things can get pretty messy at Electrowerkz – and that's just how everyone wants it to stay. Club nights include the notorious Slimelight on Saturdays, the biggest goth night in London. You have to apply for membership by showing your face at the door. Although the venue is just off the City Road, the club has the air of a warehouse rave. ⊖ Angel

Fabric

Nightclub

77a Charterhouse St, EC1   7336 8898

Fabric has always been at the cutting edge of music fashion in London. The club has opted for a minimalist mood, making room for serious dance space. The sound system in the two massive main rooms will make every cell in your body shake to drum and bass, hip-hop, electro and house. It gets packed, but if you want to hide away from the mass you can squeeze up the stairs to the little attic room and lose yourself. Tickets range from £12 to £15. ⊖ ⇄ Farringdon

Plastic People

Nightclub

147-149 Curtain Rd, EC2   7739 6471

This little basement club prides itself on hosting some of the most progressive club nights, with R'n'B, drum and bass, hip-hop, broken beats, future jazz and techno taking centre stage throughout the week. Fridays see the Future Sound of the Underground do their Forward night and DJ Abdul Forsyth and guests run Balance on Saturdays. The place is packed every weekend. ⊖ ⇄ Liverpool Street

South Bank

A decade of investment has turned this once grey no-man's land into a mish-mash of the swanky and the scruffy. Here you'll find bankers and geezers rubbing shoulders, just a stone's throw away from the river Thames.

Baltic

74 Blackfriars Rd, SE1

European
7928 1111

If the idea of the Baltic conjures up images of ice then you'll be blown away by the warm atmosphere at this restaurant. Amber walls, golden chandeliers and red paintings set a rich tone for sophisticated diners. You can enjoy a well-slung cocktail or one of more than 40 vodkas at the bar while you wait for your table. Then, once in the large, sky-lit restaurant, there are blinis and caviars available for any taste or budget, and an intricate, exotic menu. The wild boar is notable. ⊖ Southwark

Butlers Wharf Chop House

36e Shad Thames, SE1

British
7403 3403

Homegrown produce is cooked to perfection in this delightfully relaxed restaurant overlooking Tower Bridge. Wood pigeon and Cornish razor clams are among the delectable starters, followed by dishes of hearty comfort food. Butlers has not minimised any of the charm or intense flavours of these rustic favourites, but still made them accessible and appealing to urbanites. ⊖ Tower Hill

Roast, in Borough Market

Mesón don Felipe
Spanish
53 The Cut, SE1
7928 3237

In a corner of Southwark sits one of the oldest tapas restaurants in London. Adding to the hubbub of noisy diners is the sound of classical Spanish guitarists on a small stage. The service is fast and the turnover big, but the staff know exactly what it takes to ensure their guests leave happy and don't push you to move on. ⊖≷ Waterloo

Roast
British
The Floral Hall, Stoney St, SE1
7940 1300

Based in the elegant flower hall of Borough Market, Roast offers views of St Paul's and narrow, winding streets. The menu here reflects the best of British produce. Orkney rare-breed beef, tender lamb shanks and roast game are masterfully cooked and served without pretension. You can even ask for a dollop of mustard, mint sauce or horseradish on the side. Afternoon tea, served from 13:30 to 17:30, is also a delight ⊖ Southwark

The Market Porter
Pub
9 Stoney St, SE1
7407 2495

Market workers have been coming to this pub for generations. Open from 06:00, it has as much character as the most chipper 'barrow boy'. It's busy after work hours, and traders, tourists and locals crowd in on Fridays and Saturdays when Borough Market is open. Drinks are sold at proper pub prices too, rather than the inflated bar prices that you'll find in most London establishments. ⊖≷ London Bridge

Wine Wharf

Bar

Stoney St, Borough Market, SE1   7940 8335

The Wine Wharf is a modern bar with exposed brick, metal, and wooden beams that give it a characteristic warehouse feel. You can have a five glass tasting session for £10, and staff are passionate about wine and happy to share all they know. There are also a few imported beers and brandies. There's a full lunch menu alongside the usual nuts and nibbles.

⊖ ≷ London Bridge

Zacudia

Bar

River Level, 2a Southwark Bridge Rd, SE1   7021 0085

Here you can sip a 'Southwark sling' while looking out over St Paul's and the Thames. This light, clean-cut bar gets busy in the evenings with city slickers and cultured types who have come straight from the neighbouring Tate Modern. Resident DJs play soul, jazz, funk, hip-hop and house on Thursday, Friday and Saturday nights. ⊖ ≷ London Bridge

Ministry of Sound

Nightclub

103 Gaunt St, SE1   7740 8728

This legendary club retains a big following and string of homegrown and international DJ talent. Ministry is still the biggest brand in clubbing, delivering where it counts: the dancefloor. The crowd is hands-in-the-air happy until 07:00 at weekends and 05:00 on Wednesdays. The club is loyal to those who helped make it, so there are special nights for all those old ravers. If you're a Cristal clubber, you can book a table in the VIP lounge for the night. ⊖ Elephant & Castle

North London has plenty of variety in its bars and restaurants, from the leafy streets of Primrose Hill to the rowdy strip of Islington's Upper Street and the music Mecca of Camden.

Cuba Libre
72 Upper St, N1

Latin American
7354 9998

Cuba Libra packs in the crowds for classic cocktails, music and food from the largest and most individual of the Caribbean islands. The eclectic menu is not particularly authentic, but does great Caribbean and Latino-influenced dishes. Tapas and paella are the most popular with groups who have come to eat, drink and be very merry. Hover by the small bar for delicious mojitos after dinner and it won't be long before your hips shake to the salsa beats. ⊖ Angel

Fifteen
15 Westland Place, N1

Italian
0871 330 1515

Jamie Oliver's famous restaurant is still buzzing long after the hype surrounding his TV programme died down. The concept for the show and restaurant was to give 15 young wannabe chefs from disadvantaged backgrounds a chance to build a career in catering. The trattoria has a typically relaxed vibe and serves simple rustic food while downstairs is the fine-dining Mediterranean restaurant where the decor is a mix of New York subway and Tate Modern. ⊖ ⇌ Old Street

Mem and Laz

8 Theberton St, N1

Mediterranean
7704 9089

Take a great big breath as you walk in and smell the meat sizzling on the grill. The Turkish owners do what they know best – kebabs, grills and fresh fish steaks. It's heaving on Friday and Saturday nights and busy with locals even in the late afternoon, but still feels intimate enough for a romantic dinner for two. ⊖ Angel

Odette's

130 Regents Park Rd, NW1

European
7586 5486

Odette's is a Primrose Hill classic, with huge baskets of flowers, tables on the pavement in summer and a small conservatory. The menu offers modern European cuisine with a light French accent, all elegantly presented and accompanied by a wine list with choices to suit different budgets. The restaurant is one favourite that's likely to be around for a while longer. ⊖ Baker Street

The Elk in the Woods

37 Camden Passage, N1

Pub
7226 3535

Find this treasure of a tiny pub surrounded by antique shops and quirky boutiques in Camden Passage, then grab a laid-back brunch or just tuck yourself in for an afternoon of drinking in one of its big armchairs. With waiter service you won't even have to disturb yourself to go to the bar. The gastropub-style menu offers slightly unusual dishes along with the best of modern British. It can get a bit cramped, but this just adds to the convivial atmosphere. ⊖ Angel

The King's Head

Pub

115 Upper St, N1 — 7226 1916

Drop in any day of the week and you'll be entertained, not just by the musicians performing from 22:00, but also by the actors and comedians who have made this place their second home. The old saying 'if it ain't broke don't fix it' applies here, to the Victorian cash register still pinging behind the bar and the venue itself. ⊖ Angel

Bar Vinyl

Bar

6 Inverness St, NW1 — 7681 7898

Music lovers come to this legendary bar to drink and flick through the record collection of its award-winning basement shop. It has a relaxed mood during the day, when DJs start playing from 14:00, and staff help keep things lively later, pulling Hoegarden and Budvar by the gallon. The reasonably priced menu offers simple but tasty food, from salads and ciabatta sandwiches to fresh pizzas. ⊖ Camden

The Big Chill House

Bar

257-259 Pentonville Rd, N1 — 7684 2019

As its name suggests, this friendly and relaxed bar attracts a young crowd keen to hear chilled dance music and enjoy a few drinks. It's big, with three floors of dance and drinking space, and the layout encourages groups to mix, mingle and lounge. There is a terrace which is perfect when you want to get some fresh air, though many might argue that the air down busy Pentonville Road is anything but fresh.

⊖ King's Cross St. Pancras

Medicine Bar

Bar

181 Upper St, N1   7704 8056

One of the forerunners of the DJ-bar concept, laid-back
Medicine has a following of firm believers. The music and
atmosphere is plugged in, but not in-your-face, and the
crowds really go for it at the weekend. The temperature rises
on the dancefloor and upstairs, so the bar gets phenomenally
packed; staff do their best to keep up but it can take a while
to get served. ⊖ Angel

Barfly

Nightclub

49 Chalk Farm Rd, NW1   7691 4244

An institution in the music world, Barfly is one of the hottest
places to see soon-to-be-big new bands. The bare brick walls
still manage to be battered every night of the week by the
savvy crowds who come in to see some of the 1,000-plus live
acts that play every year. The bar staff try their best to hear
your order over the music, but you'll have to shout at least
three times. ⊖ Camden

The Underworld

Nightclub

174 Camden High St, NW1   7482 1932

Directly opposite Camden tube station and tucked under
the World's End pub is a club that has become as famous as
the prodigious bands that have graced its stage. Whatever
the night, The Underworld can be relied on for a great
atmosphere, big crowd and scruffy, down to earth fun. You
can get tickets for its numerous gigs from the pub upstairs.
⊖ Camden

North London

South London

Don't let yourself miss a night south of the river. From the proper poshness of Fulham, to the bedlam of Brixton, south London has plenty of undiscovered hotspots that most tourists miss.

Bamboula
Caribbean
12 Acre Lane, SW2
7737 6633

This small, charming Caribbean restaurant showcases tasty foods that will make you want to come back. This is unpretentious fare served with a smile, with reggae playing to keep the staff moving. If you've got a big appetite you can guarantee 'satisfaction' with the namesake menu, but if it's gargantuan you could try the 'hungry man' option. ⊖ Brixton

Bar du Musee
European
17 Nelson Rd, SE10
8858 4710

Bar du Musee has French styling, staff, and ambience, but offers a modern European menu. The bar serves wine by the glass from an extensive list, as well as cigars and food to a jazz soundtrack. In summer you can easily spend a lazy day under the of one of the white canopy umbrellas. **DLR** Cutty Sark

Bluebird Dining Room
British
350 King's Rd, SW3
7559 1129

Fresh, clean design is at the core of the beautiful first-floor dining room of Sir Terence Conran's Bluebird Brasserie. It is

obvious after just one mouthful that the ingredients, sourced from small farms and producers across the British Isles, are of the highest quality. And what could be more authentic than Cornish crab, crackled pork or a knickerbocker glory?

⊖ South Kensington

The Hill
European

89 Royal Hill, SE10
8691 3626

Tucked into the corner of a backstreet in central Greenwich is The Hill, a beautiful pub and restaurant with a lovely garden. Come for drinks at the bar, sip a good cup of coffee while admiring the oil paintings for sale, or sit at one of the tables in the raised section of the brasserie for a delicious lunch or dinner. **DLR** ⇌ Greenwich

Coopers Arms
Pub

87 Flood St, SW3
7376 3120

This Victorian-style backstreet pub has plenty of charm and a relaxed atmosphere, ideal for a Sunday reading the papers by the fire while nursing a pint of ale. The food is modern European and good quality for the money. The open bar area feels light and airy, and the plants and pine furniture add a sense of space. ⊖ South Kensington

The Gipsy Moth
Pub

60 Greenwich Church St, SE10
8858 0786

Just opposite the Cutty Sark, this pub's big garden is a hit in the summer – but it's a pity that it closes at 21:30. The conservatory is delicately lit with fairy lights, but the menu is a far more macho affair with chicken and ham pie and sausage sandwich with roasted red onion among the dishes on offer. **DLR** Cutty Sark

The Pig's Ear
Pub

35 Old Church St, SW3
7352 2908

A good-looking boozer for good-looking people, The Pig's Ear has made a fine job of bringing pub culture into the 21st century. As long as you're not on a budget you'll have a fantastic time. At night it gets busy with a very Chelsea crowd, but in the day it has a relaxed vibe. ⊖ South Kensington

The Fridge
Nightclub

1 Town Hall Parade, SW2
7326 5100

This lovingly restored 1930s building is home to one of London's longest-running independent clubs. Look out for the fridges over the front doors, go-go dancers, and TV screens hanging from the ceiling. All kinds of people, from gay to straight and everything in between, mix it up on the floor to big-name DJs, who play every night. ⊖ Brixton

Mass
Nightclub

St Matthews Church, Brixton Hill, SW2
7738 7875

This spacious club, a converted church, has a reputation for hard and heavy underground music, from R'n'B and house right through to trance and grime. Three large rooms usually fill up quickly for the various club nights, which include Torture Garden. Drinks are reasonable and the entrance fee not too outrageous for such wicked, sinful nights. ⊖ Brixton

West London

It's a little more placid than other parts of town, but west London has actually been home to a swinging music scene since the 60s and entertained high society for even longer.

12th House
European
35 Pembridge Rd, W11
7727 9620

Enjoy a drink downstairs in this astrological hang-out or head upstairs where the restaurant serves out-of-this-world lamb shank. Sharing platters are fun to nibble on while you prepare for your astrology and tarot readings to be done by an expert. If you don't have a full chart, staff will ask you your star sign and give you a card with your horoscope on. ⊖ Notting Hill Gate

Gordon Ramsay at Claridge's
European
Claridge's, Brook St, W1
7499 0099

The staff herehave charm and charisma, a rarity in fine-dining restaurants. A set lunch offers three courses for £30, which is great value for exquisite cuisine. Head chef Mark Sargeant watches over proceedings, and you can even request a seat in the the kitchen at the chef's table while enjoying an eight-course tasting menu tailored just for you. ⊖ Bond Street

Kanteen
European
K West Hotel and Spa, Richmond Way, W1   0870 0274343

Contemporary chic sets the scene for suitably modern cuisine. The express menu is popular for lunch and if you don't get your starter, main course and coffee served within an hour it's free. In the evenings, dining is rather more indulgent, before guests drink all through the night in the 24 hour K Bar lounge. ⊖ Shepherd's Bush

Maggie Jones's   British
6 Old Court Place, Kensington Church St, W8   7937 6462
This is homely British cooking in a simple but sophisticated restaurant. The decor is quaint and faintly eccentric, but expect to find skillfully cooked classics such as potted shrimp, haunch of venison and game pies, as well as a variety of dishes cooked to traditional recipes using fresh, regional produce. ⊖ High Street Kensington

Notting Grill   British
123a Clarendon Rd, W11   7229 1500
TV chef Antony Worrall Thompson has created a relaxed dining room serving simple British fare for foodies. Starters include plenty of 1980s restaurant classics while main courses are meat focused. There are no chef secrets here, just a sincere care for what you are eating. You can even find out the provenance of all of the organic, locally sourced produce.
⊖ Notting Hill Gate

Pétrus   French
The Berkeley, Wilton Place, SW1   7235 1200
Dining at Pétrus feels more like an invitation to an opulent stately home than a night at a restaurant. The senses are excited by the impressive wine list and modern French cuisine,

imaginatively created by top chef Marcus Wareing. If you think it's too good to be true, you're welcome to go in to the kitchen to meet the chefs and see the action. ⊖ Knightsbridge

The Castle
Pub

225 Portobello Rd, W11
7221 7103

The Castle is a refreshingly dark, rough-around-the-edges little pub. The entertainment is top notch, with live music on Wednesdays in the form of acoustic, rock, hip-hop and rap acts. Customers turn DJ on Thursdays with the 'bring your own records' night. The kitchen offers standard pub dishes such as burgers, sandwiches, roasts, and a few other deviations, which are very well turned out. ⊖ Ladbroke Grove

Earl of Lonsdale
Pub

277-281 Westbourne Grove, W11
7727 6335

Instead of being stripped and refurbished, this place has recreated an 'olde worlde' pub, thankfully without becoming a parody of itself. The food is good, staff are helpful and the drinks are reasonably priced, with plenty of ales and bitters on offer. There are open fires in the back room for a winter's day and a lovely garden for the summer months.
⊖ Notting Hill Gate

Prince Albert
Pub

11 Pembridge Rd, W11
7727 7362

Near Notting Hill tube station you'll find one of the best pubs in the area. You can nibble on its well priced bar snacks or order organic food prepared in the open kitchen. There's an impressive selection of Belgian beers with strawberry Frülli on tap. A huge chandelier hangs from the ceiling but The Prince Albert remains remarkably dark, especially the back room.

⊖ Notting Hill Gate

Cherry Jam
Bar

58 Porchester Rd, W2 — 7727 9950

At the weekend things get hot in this cherry-red venue, with tunes from samba to house, electro and soul. Once a month, the legendary Book Slam takes place, where novelist and hip-hop journalist Patrick Neate hosts an evening of literature, music and spoken-word performances. ⊖ Royal Oak

Neighbourhood
Nightclub

12 Acklam Rd, W10 — 89609331

The triple-stack turntables at Neighbourhood have been worked by the hands of some of the best DJs in the industry. This isn't a sweaty, hardcore club; people seem to look out for each other. Spread over two floors, it has a sociable, fun atmosphere and you'll wish it was in your neighbourhood.

⊖ Notting Hill Gate

Notting Hill Arts Club
Nightclub

21 Notting Hill Gate, W11 — 7460 4459

You'll find diverse acts here every night of the week. There are live gigs and DJ sets playing Scandinavian sounds, alternative hip-hop, break beats, indie, punk, soul and groove. It's open until 02:00 seven nights a week. If you're in before 18:00 it's free, after that you can expect to pay about £5. ⊖ Notting Hill Gate

East London

London's once derelict East End has been reborn as artists, trendies and new media types converged to create a cutting edge atmosphere and some bohemian nightlife.

Drunken Monkey

Chinese

222 Shoreditch High St, E1
7392 9606

Silk lanterns and purple neon lighting create a suitably cool setting for this den of excellent dining. Open until midnight, it's a great place to swill cocktails and share baskets of fabulous dumplings, buns and spring rolls or generous portions of noodles. There is a happy hour every day and regular special offers on drinks, but the focus is on the marvellous food. ⊖ ⇄ Old Street

E Pellicci

Cafe

332 Bethnal Green Rd, E2
7739 4873

Once a meeting place for the notorious Kray brothers and their gang, this is an unmistakable and unforgettable East End cafe. Owner Nevio Pellicci and his son know almost all of the people who come through the door and seem genuinely enthused to see them. Generations have been coming for killer breakfasts, egg and chips or just a mug of tea. Outside, the cafe's original lettering and a red neon sign hang overhead, while inside the open, intricate art deco-style wooden interior is a delight. ⊖ ⇄ Bethnal Green

Patisserie Valerie
Cafe

Bishop Square, 37 Brushfield St, E1   7247 4906

It's hard not to notice the fabulous cakes and sweet creations in the window of this beautiful, family-run Italian cafe and patisserie. The ciabatta bar is great for a takeaway, the coffee is superb and the staff are friendly and animated. The 60 seat brasserie is open until 20:00 and is great for a quick dinner after a hard day's work. ⊖ ⇌ Liverpool Street

S&M Café
Cafe

48 Brushfield St, E1   7247 2252

There's nothing kinky going on at this 1950s style cafe, unless grilled sausages and mash do it for you. You can order from a range of more than 20 varieties of sausage, four types of fluffy mash and three gravies, accompanied by mugs of tea or something a bit stronger. Finish with apple crumble served with custard 'just like grandma used to make'. This is comfort food of the first order. ⊖ ⇌ Liverpool Street

Frizzante@City Farm
Cafe

Hackney City Farm, 1a Goldsmith's Row, E2   7739 2266

From farm to table in under 100 metres – you can't get fresher free-range eggs with your toast than this. Popular with families, Frizzante serves Mediterranean cuisine and cafe staples. This is the perfect place to bring children (and adults) who are too used to seeing their food sliced and shrink wrapped. There are plenty of vegetarian options plus a seasonally changing specials menu and heavenly desserts. ⊖ Bethnal Green

Commercial Tavern
142-144 Commercial St, E1

Pub

7247 1888

Cabbages serve as candlestick holders in the eccentrically refurbished Commercial Tavern. Its outrageously flamboyant owners have lovingly added their own quirky sense of style and a welcoming atmosphere. In an era of chain pubs and themed bars it's fantastic to see something a bit different, and the from polka dot tables and myriad mirrors certainly do that. And with tunes playing from Elvis to *The Sound of Music*, it's pretty clear that no-one is trying to take themselves too seriously. ⊖ ⇄ Old Street

Owl and Pussycat
34 Redchurch St, E2

Pub

7613 3628

This 16th-century boozer has survived modernisation in Shoreditch. There is a huge open fire and even a traditional bar billiards table. Good pub food is offered, with a carvery upstairs and tables in the garden at the back make a lovely place to sip a drink in the summer. Be quick though, it's only small and its reputation is spreading fast. ⊖ ⇄ Old Street

Loungelover
1 Whitby St, E2

Bar

7012 1234

Flamboyant, artistic and decadent, this is a favourite among east London trendies. The interior is filled with chandeliers, hippo heads, gilt mirrors and lush velvet. The cocktails are exceptionally good (if a little expensive) and the canape menu, which includes wild boar, is suitably glamorous. The bar operates a fairly tight booking system. ⊖ ⇄ Liverpool Street

Visitor Info

Getting Around

Getting around in London is no problem. From the famous tube to the ubiquitous black cabs, you can get from A to B in numerous ways.

Although not based around a grid system as found in other cities, London is still remarkably easy to navigate, and the public transport system is excellent, both in terms of variety and quality. London has one of the oldest and most comprehensive public transportation systems in the world, more buses on the roads than ever before, is teeming with the iconic black cabs with their knowledgeable drivers, and is home to the underground system (or tube, as it is more commonly known).

Further improvements are promised in the run-up to the 2012 Olympic Games, including expansion of the underground in London's currently neglected East End, and a tram system running from north to south.

The capital is not so great if you plan to drive your own car. What with congestion charges deterring drivers from central London and the extortionately priced and meagre parking facilities, over-zealous wardens and high penalties, driving in the city is best avoided.

Transport for London (TfL) has an extensive website providing up-to-the-minute information on all modes of London transport. The Journey Planner section is particularly worth a browse for you to map out the best routes to and from specific locations, by rail, tube, bus, and

bicycle or on foot (visit www.tfl.gov.uk/journeyplanner).
There's also a network of Travel Information Centres located
at various stations throughout the city, including Piccadilly
Circus, Heathrow Airport, Victoria and Liverpool Street.

Air

International flights to London arrive at Heathrow (LHR),
Gatwick (LGW), Stansted (STN),
Luton (LTN) or City Airport (LCY).

City, Luton and the state-of-
the-art Stansted (designed by
Sir Norman Foster) are mainly
served by European airlines,
and no-frills carriers such as
Ryanair and easyJet. The rise
of low-cost airlines has meant
domestic flights from London
to Scotland and cities in the
north of the UK are now a viable
alternative to train travel.

Rail

Overland trains are useful for
reaching places that are not
served by the tube, whether it's
a little out of London or further
afield. These services tend to
be less regular than the tube
and some are not covered by

When You Land

**There are excellent bus
and train connections
between airports and the
city centre. Trains can be
quick, especially on the
Gatwick and Heathrow
Express services, but
you'll have to get yourself
and your luggage to the
carriage. Airport link buses
(generally National Express
Airport buses) may ease
the luggage factor and
drop you closer to central
hotels, but they're subject
to London traffic, which can
be horrid. Taxis can be more
convenient than buses, but
you pay for efficiency.**

Avoid getting old ahead of time.
[www.laythemflat.co.uk]

the Oyster card system. Mainline stations include Waterloo, London Bridge and Victoria, serving the south of England; Paddington, serving the west; King's Cross and Euston, serving the north; and Liverpool Street, serving the east. Tickets must be bought before boarding. A good tip is to book your tickets as far in advance as possible; the earlier you buy, the cheaper ticket.

Taxi

The famous black cab now comes in different colours. If you're not at a designated rank, there's no etiquette to follow: a yellow light above the windscreen indicates that the cab is available, just stick your arm out to signal it or be bold and jump straight in (if you don't, someone else will, particularly at night when cabs are scarce). The meter starts at £2.20 and increases in increments of 20p for each 219 metres. Just so you know, drivers may refuse to take you if your destination is too far from the centre or, in many cases, their home. It is standard to round up to the nearest pound as a tip.

Minicabs are an alternative to black cabs, and must display their licences in their car. They can't be hailed from the street, and must be hired by phone or directly from one of the many 24 hour minicab offices around the city. As they are unmetered, it is important to fix the price in advance, otherwise your trip could be an expensive one.

Avoid Like The Plague

However tempting, unlicensed (and illegal) minicab drivers touting for fares should be avoided, particularly by those travelling alone.

London Underground

Endearingly referred to as the tube (trains are cylindrical), the London Underground was the first urban underground transportation system in the world (though almost 55% of the tracks are actually above ground). Services started in January 1863 and since then carriages have moved some 100 million people across London. There are 12 underground lines, plus the Docklands Light Railway and interconnected overland stations, all marked in different colours on Harry Beck's famous map. The first train operates at around 05:00, Monday to Saturday and around 07:30 on Sunday. The last train leaves between 23:30 and 00.30. A standard single ticket within Zones 1 to 4 costs £3, while travelling from Zone 5 or 6 to Zone 1 will cost £4. The network can get uncomfortably busy during rush hour and it's worth bearing in mind that London commuters are hard nosed when it comes to tube etiquette. Anyone standing on the left side of

Congestion Charge

This TfL levy, rolled out to much controversy and criticism in 2003, charges motorists £5 (now £8) every time they head into central London between 07:00 and 18:30, Monday to Friday. The charge was introduced to cut back on the number of cars in the city, reduce pollution and encourage more people to use public transport. Look out for the red C signs painted on the ground and on posts warning drivers that they are about to enter the charging zone. Failure to pay the charge means a fine of at least £50.

the escalator is likely to be given a cold stare; stand on the right and you'll be fine. For more information visit www.tfl.gov.uk/tube.

Bus

London's network of buses can seem quite complex, but once you get used to hopping on and off, it's quite easy to navigate – and a great way to sightsee and get your bearings. The majority of the capital's buses are distinctive red double-deckers – although they're all now modern versions, as the famous Routemasters went out of service in 2005. Bus stops are conveniently allocated and pretty easy to spot. At every stop you'll find a schedule as well as the bus route itself. A network of night buses is also available.

Cycling

London is in the grip of a bike revolution. There are now some 450,000 cyclists on the capital's roads per day,

Easier Oysters

If you're travelling several times in one day or through a couple of zones, you should consider a Travelcard or Oyster card. An all-day Travelcard will allow you unlimited access to all underground stations as well as busses in the zones you have paid for. An Oyster card is a reusable electronic version, which works on a 'pay as you go' system. There is no time limit on the value on your card and you can add more money as and when you need to. Using an Oyster card will get you discounted rates on your journey.

but pedalling in the city centre is not for the faint-hearted; despite being a quick, cheap and healthy mode of moving about. Ongoing efforts are making cycling even easier and more enjoyable, including the introduction of additional bicycle lanes. For information on cycle routes, see www.tfl.gov.uk/cycles. Although not required by law, it's a good idea to wear a helmet and visible clothing, and a face mask if the smog bothers you.

Walking

When it comes to really seeing London, there's nothing better than putting your best foot forward and taking to the streets. Apart from all the fresh air, you'll also get to pass landmarks often missed when you travel by tube. Walking can also save you time: for instance, if you wanted to travel from Great Portland Street to Regent's Park, you'd have to take two separate trains – even though the two stations are actually only metres apart. The Mayor of London has expressed his commitment to making the capital one of the most walking friendly cities in the world and plans are already underway to improve the pedestrian environment. Remember, cars drive on the left in the UK so make sure you look the 'right' way when crossing the road.

Time Traveller

The Transport Museum in Covent Garden is a brilliant place to spend a rainy afternoon, with some incredibly elaborate and fascinating displays tracking the transportation history of this great city.

Essential Info

This section contains all the practical info you ever needed to know about London, no matter how long you're staying.

Disabled Visitors

Thanks to the Disability Discrimination Act of 1995, all new tourist attractions and hotels must make full provision for wheelchair users, and access to public places has greatly improved. Unfortunately, many of London's older buildings are yet to be upgraded for people with special needs. However, many of these places, such as museums, make extra efforts for individual requirements. This can include wheelchairs for free hire, signed shows, induction loops and Braille guides.

Modernisation of The Victorian-era London Underground network has been challenging, and access to most stations is via numerous steps. Newer routes, such as the Jubilee Line, do have more stations with a lift service though, and almost 100% of London Buses are wheelchair accessible.

The national blue badge scheme that allows special parking for physically challenged car users has only limited application in Westminster, the City of London and parts of Kensington, Chelsea and Camden. Badge holders are not allowed to park on yellow lines in these areas during the day.

Bussiness & Social Hours

Most offices work a fixed Monday to Friday, 09:00 to 17:00 week – you only have to be on the tube during rush hour to realise how true this is. Business hours elsewhere in the city vary greatly. Shops in central London are generally open until at least 19:00 from Monday to Saturday, and until 18:00 on Sunday. Most areas offer late-night shopping on Thursdays. Some grocery stores and petrol stations are open 24 hours.

Most Londoners work around 40 hours a week, spread out over five days. Working conditions are pretty good, and most employees get an hour's break at some point in the day. There are those who work double this – although for city folk in law firms and the banking industries, the wages make it worthwhile.

Currency & Exchange Rates

Despite being a member of the EU, the UK has not signed up to the euro and has retained the pound sterling and pence as its unit of currency. One hundred pence make one pound (£1). Coins come in denominations of £2, £1, 50p, 20p, 10p, 5p, 2p and 1p, while paper notes come in denominations of £5, £10, £20 and £50. The different notes

Closing Time

Despite the much-debated extension to the capital's licensing laws, London hasn't experienced the problems and disruption that many of the UK's conservative newspapers anticipated, mainly because few pubs have greatly changed their opening hours. This means most places are usually open from midday until 23:00, and working Londoners are generally tucked up in bed by midnight. A quick pint after work is popular with most, with heavy partying saved for the weekend.

are quite similar in size and appearance, so be careful. It's not common to see a £50 so they are often scrutinised. Scottish banks issue their own bank notes of the same values but they are interchangeable in England. People often abbreviate, so if something that costs £2.50, you'd say it was 'two-fifty'. A 'quid' is colloquial for £1. For things that cost less than a pound, people may say 'pence'.

You can change cash and travellers' cheques at banks, post offices, large travel agents, some Tourist Information Centres, American Express and bureaux de change outlets throughout the city – just bring some proof of identity with you. Banks and travel agents will usually charge a fixed fee, about 3%, with a minimum fee of £2.50. Post offices, however, don't charge any commission. If it's not convenient to go to a post office, the exchanges TTT Foreign Exchange Corporation and Thomas Exchange Global both have several branches in the centre of town.

i

For What It's Worth

Considered one of the hard currencies, the pound is now free flowing (so not tagged to any other currency, like certain countries to the US dollar). This means that it can be bought and sold on the stock exchange and that its value is relative to the economic market and other currencies (going up when traders are buying pounds and down when they're selling them).

Money

Every area of London has at least one of the big high-street banks (NatWest, Lloyds TSB, HSCB and Royal Bank of Scotland).

The opening hours for most are Monday to Friday, 09:30 to 16:30, although some in central London are open till 17:00 during the week and on Saturday mornings. Several of these banks have international status, or at least affiliation with equivalent banks abroad, and you can exchange travellers' cheques and currencies within them at a fairly low commission.

Even more prolific are the ATMs on almost every street. These accept Visa, MasterCard, Cirrus or Maestro cards. They can be a cheap way of drawing out British currency as they work on a good exchange rate. There is normally a fee charged to credit cards used in this way and your bank may also charge you a fee for withdrawing money.

Most hotels, shops and restaurants in London accept major credit cards such as MasterCard, Visa, American Express and Diners Club. In smaller shops and restaurants, it's worth checking whether they accept credit cards before placing your order.

Debit cards are becoming very popular, overtaking cash as the main way to spend money. In 2005, debit card usage in the UK overtook cash, with £89 billion being spent

i Plastic Safety

Card cloning is on the increase nationally where skimming devices have been attached to ATMs. With the advent of Chip & PIN cards, it is now very difficult to use cloned cards for retail sales. However, it is still possible to use them to get cash from ATMs, so you should check the ATM carefully before using it and shield the screen or keypad when tapping in your PIN.

on cards in shops, stores, supermarkets and online. Your debit card will also allow you to get cash from most ATMs, as well as 'cash back' from leading supermarkets.

Telephone & Internet

London's traditional red phone boxes are now tourist sights in their own right – although most have been replaced by BT (British Telecom) versions. Most take coins, phone cards and credit cards. Pre-paid phone cards, sold in denominations of £5, £10, £15 and £20, can be bought from selected newsagents.

BT have pinned their future survival on the fact that it is also possible to check and send emails from public phones, although it can be expensive.

London is increasingly net-friendly – many hotel rooms have internet access and there are also a huge number of cyber cafes all over the city. The biggest and easiest to use are part of the easyEverything chain (www.easyeverything. com), which has locations all over central London, starting at £1 for 30 minutes. Keep an eye on your belongings while you surf though, as pickpocketing is rife.

For laptop users, most of the large hotels offer free WiFi access. Larger coffee shop

Just To Say

You can find public BT phoneboxes on every street corner in London, where you can pay for calls by cash or credit card. Other operators can also install phone points and phone boxes, which are operated in a similar way. Emergency calls to 999 are always free.

chains, such as Starbucks, charge for the service, but several smaller cafes and pubs offer it for free to get customers in. Look for a sign in the window or ask.

Newspapers

The UK is home to numerous media outlets, most of which are based in London (perhaps fuelling accusations of a 'London bias' in the national press).

The national daily newspapers are divided into two main categories: 'broadsheets', such as *The Guardian*, *Daily Telegraph* and *Independent*, which have extensive foreign coverage and home news; and 'tabloids', such as *The Sun*, *The Mirror*, *The Daily Mail*, *Daily Express* and *The Star*, which do cover major news stories but tend to focus on celebrity, scandal and entertainment. Newspapers are available at all newsstands and newsagents throughout the city (and most hotels by request), and cost less than £1 during the week. The price rises on weekends when many supplements are included, such as TV guides, listings and, with the broadsheets, high-quality glossy magazines.

London also has its own four city-wide daily newspaper titles; the paid-for *Evening Standard* (sister paper of the *Daily Mail*), plus three free papers, *Metro*, *London Lite* and *The London Paper*, all of which are available on the streets, and at tube and railway stations. The independent weekly listings magazine *Time Out* is a valuable source of information

American and European newspapers are available in central London at good newsagents and the larger news stands and cost a fraction more than at home. Antipodeans have their own UK-based weekly magazine, *TNT*, which contains home news as well as London job and accommodation listings and is available outside many central tube stations.

Crime & Safety

Central London's crime rate isn't considered to be especially high; the violent crime rate is 22.2 per 1,000 people. Gun crime is creeping up, although this has so far been restricted to inner-city areas. Crime is more likely to be of the petty kind, so when using an ATM, check that no one is looking over your shoulder and make sure your wallet and phone are kept out of sight when not in use (many pubs have clips under the tables to secure bags). Leaving your bag unattended could also lead to security alerts.

CCTV covers most of Oxford Street and the West End and is monitored 24/7 by trained officers, but you should still use common sense, especially at night. Stick to well-lit areas and be careful not to flash around large wads of money or expensive items. There are a number of unlicensed mini-cabs, which may try and offer you a cheaper fare, but they should be avoided. While public transport is safe, especially since the increased police presence in underground stations, you need to keep your eye on your belongings.

London's police force is the Metropolitan Police, known as 'The Met'. There are over 30,000 officers operating in the capital, including members of the British Transport Police, who are responsible for preventing crime on trains and the London Underground. The Met also has a division that patrols the Thames in speedboats.

The City of London has its own police force, responsible for the Square Mile. The forces are separate, but wear similar navy blue uniforms, as do City Guardians and Police Community Support Officers (PCSOs), who patrol throughout London. All officers are approachable, friendly and very helpful.

Visas & Customs

Citizens of EU countries to the UK can come and go as they please. Citizens of the USA, Canada, Australia, South Africa and New Zealand only require a valid passport for a visit of up to six months. Citizens from other countries need to apply for a visa, regardless of how long they are planning to visit the UK for. For more information on the visa process, and to find out whether you need to apply for a visa, visit www.ukvisas. gov.uk. Recent terrorist attacks have seen a tightening of the visa process, so it's worth double checking the correct procedure based on your nationality as in some cases the visa process takes time. Once you have your visa, it is important to know about Britain's customs rules. There are two systems: one for goods bought duty free, and one for goods bought

Free Goodies

For goods purchased at airports or on ferries outside the EU, you are allowed to import 200 cigarettes, 50 cigars or 250g of tobacco. You are allowed two litres of still wine, plus one litre of spirits (over 22%) or another two litres of wine (sparkling or otherwise). You are allowed to bring in 50g of perfume, 250cc of eau de toilette, as well as other duty free goods to the value of £145.

in another EU country where taxes and duties have already been paid. Although you can't bring in duty free goods from another EU country, the majority of duty-paid goods are still cheaper outside the UK, so you can still save money. All items are meant for individual consumption only, and a customs officer will ask questions if he or she suspects that you have bought products for commercial purposes - if it is found that you have, your products will be seized and you could face further penalties.

The same applies if you are caught selling alcohol or tobacco goods, which is a serious offence and could result in up to seven years in prison.

Unlicensed drugs, offensive weapons, indecent and obscene material featuring children, counterfeit and pirated goods, meat, dairy and other animal products are prohibited from being brought into the UK from any destinations.

Tourist Information

London's main tourist office is the Britain and London Visitor Centre at Lower Regent Street (0870 1566366), near the Picadilly Circus tube station. It is open seven days a week, from 09:00 to 18:30 on weekdays and from 10:00 to 16:00 at weekends (from June to September, it is open from 09:00 to 17:00 on Saturdays). The shop provides free information and travel advice for visitors to London and Britain, and can offer assistance with booking tickets, accommodation and transport. A similar service is available from the London Information Centre in Leicester Square (7292 2333). See www.visitbritain.com for a full list of tourist information offices.

Places to Stay

Whether you simply want an inn for the night or are looking for a luscious spot for a romantic weekend, London offers a range of accommodation to suit your needs and budget.

Although London can be pricey, it is packed full of accommodation for every taste and budget. According to the latest figures from Visit London, there are 564 hotels and 165,846 beds, with occupancy rates high enough to make advance booking recommended. At the top end of the market there are several world-renowned five-star hotels such as The Ritz, The Savoy, The Dorchester and Claridge's, where you can expect a few famous faces.

For those with a lighter purse, hostel accommodation across London has improved greatly, with cheap digs appearing more regularly in recent years. Hotel apartments also offer a cheaper alternative to hotels for families, large groups or those on short-term work contracts. Not only that, but they also allow visitors the chance to feel more at home; most come complete with kitchens, linen and dining areas. Apartment accommodation ranges from luxury serviced suites such as the Athenaeum in the heart of Mayfair (www. athenaeumhotel.com), to shared options such as Alexander Fleming House (www.studystay.com) in Hoxton, which is comprised of self-contained flats. Prices are more competitive than they used to be, but it's always best to compare various online sources before booking.

The Savoy

www.fairmont.com/savoy   7836 4343

The Savoy vies with The Ritz as London's most prestigious hotel. Guests have included Marilyn Monroe and various members of the royal family since the hotel was opened in 1889. Some of the hotel's 250 rooms offer great views of the Thames, and its signature restaurant, The Savoy Grill, has a Michelin star.

Claridges

www.theclaridgeshotellondon.com   7629 8860

This elegant hotel is a London institution; for over a century it has enjoyed the patronage of the world's most illustrious guests, each attracted to the huge, plush rooms and art deco flourishes. The hotel's Gordon Ramsay restaurant, a recent addition, has become an attraction in its own right.

Covent Garden Hotel

www.firmdale.com/covent.htm   7806 1000

Situated in the heart of London's theatreland and once a French hospital, this stylish hotel has become a major hangout for the film set, who often make use of the hotel's screening rooms. There are 58 individually designed bedrooms and suites, mostly with huge windows overlooking the rooftops of central London.

Hoxton Hotel

www.hoxtonhotels.com   7550 1000

Located just a short hop from both the City and Hoxton's hipster bars, this hotel impresses visitors with its sleek decor, mod cons and plump bed linen – especially as prices are more than reasonable. Small rooms cost from £59 a night with free water, fresh milk, free WiFi and phone calls charged at standard rates.

K West

www.k-west.co.uk   0870 0274343

K West Hotel in Shepherd's Bush has become the main late night hang-out for London's hip crowd and rock stars regularly stagger around on the way to bed. However, it also attracts guests from all walks of life, and the hotel's spa, K Spa, is undoubtedly one of the most stylish places in the city to relax and unwind.

The Ritz

www.theritzlondon.com   7493 8181

Standing proud since 1906, The Ritz is decadently opulent (it has its own line in fine jewellery) – and expensive. Its world-famous afternoon tea is a more reasonable, if similarly luxurious, proposition for visitors. The hotel even prides itself on having two members of staff per guest room.

One Aldwych

www.onealdwych.co.uk   7300 1000

One Aldwych has racked up the awards in its relatively short life. Housed in a Edwardian building dating from 1907, it is arguably the most cutting-edge and contemporary in the capital. As well as its collection of contemporary art – there is a piece in each of the 105 rooms – the swimming pool plays music.

Renaissance Chancery Court

www.renaissancehotels.com   7829 9888

This landmark structure, built in 1914, has only recently been turned into a hotel. And so striking is the building that it has been featured in numerous film and TV productions. But if the grand architecture doesn't floor you, the high-class facilities, including a very swish spa and restaurant, definitely will.

The Sanderson

www.sandersonlondon.com   7300 1400

The listed 60s office block that now houses the Sanderson is not the most elegant facade for a stylish boutique hotel, but Ian Schrager, the king of New York hip, has worked his magic, along with Philippe Starck. The hotel has a lush bamboo-filled roof garden, a large courtyard, spa, restaurant and several uber-hip bars.

Bed & Breakfasts

Since bed and breakfasts (B&B) are such a great British institution, London has plenty all over the city. Most are housed in former residential properties, which means rooms can be on the small side. However, they normally offer the same amenities as hotels, such as TVs, tea and coffee-making facilities and telephones, but at cheaper prices. B&Bs also normally offer a more 'intimate' experience, with the chance to chat with other guests in communal areas – which can be a plus point or down point, depending on how sociable you are.

Budget

Although it has a reputation for being expensive, London does have options for those with a lighter purse – and hostel accommodation has come a long way. Many now offer private rooms, some even with en-suite bathrooms – providing a thrifty alternative to hotels. They are also ideal for lone travellers looking to meet people, or get some ideas of what to do and see while you're in town.

Bed and Breakfasts	Number	Website
Aster House	7581 5888	www.asterhouse.com
B&B Belgravia	7259 8570	www.bb-belgravia.com
The Lord Jim Hotel	7370 6071	www.lgh-hotels.com
Budget Accomodation	Number	Website
Palmers Lodge	7483 8470	www.palmerslodge.co.uk
Hyde Park Inn	7229 0000	www.hydeparkinn.com
Astors Museum Inn	7580 5360	www.astorhostels.com

Explorer Products

Residents' Guides

All you need to know about living, working and enjoying life in these exciting destinations

 Abu Dhabi
 Amsterdam
 Bahrain
 Barcelona
 Dubai
 Dublin
 Geneva
 Hong Kong
 Kuwait
 London
 New York
 New Zealand
 Oman
 Paris
 Qatar
 Shanghai
 Singapore
 Sydney

✱ Covers not final. Titles available Winter 2007.

Mini Guides

Perfect pocket-sized
visitors' guides

* Covers not
final. Titles
available
Winter 2007.

Activity Guides

Drive, trek, dive and swim... life will never be boring again

Mini Maps

Fit the city in
your pocket

* Covers not final. Titles available Winter 2007.

Maps

Wherever you are, never get lost again

Mini Photography Books*

Beautiful cities caught through the lens

* All covers not final. Titles available Winter 2007.

Lifestyle Products & Calendars

The perfect accessories for a buzzing lifestyle

Explorer Team

Publisher
Alistair MacKenzie

Editorial
Managing Editor Claire England
Lead Editors David Quinn,
Jane Roberts, Matt Farquharson,
Sean Kearns, Tim Binks
Deputy Editors Helen Spearman,
Katie Drynan, Tom Jordan
Editorial Assistants Ingrid Cupido,
Mimi Stankova

Design
Creative Director Pete Maloney
Art Director Ieyad Charaf
Senior Designers Alex Jeffries,
Motaz Al Bunai
Layout Manager Jayde Fernandes
Designers Hashim Moideen,
Rafi Pullat, Shefeeq Marakkatepurath,
Sunita Lakhiani
Cartography Manager
Zainudheen Madathil
Cartographer Noushad Madathil
Design Admin Manager
Shyrell Tamayo
Production Coordinator
Maricar Ong

Photography
Photography Manager
Pamela Grist
Photographer Victor Romero
Image Editor Henry Hilos

Sales and Marketing
Area Sales Managers Laura Zuffa,
Stephen Jones
Marketing Manager Kate Fox
Retail Sales Manager
Ivan Rodrigues
Retail Sales Coordinator
Kiran Melwani
Distribution Executives
Abdul Gafoor, Ahmed Mainodin
Firos Khan, Mannie Lugtu
Warehouse Assistant Mohammed
Kunjaymo
Drivers Mohammed Sameer,
Shabsir Madathil

Finance and Administration
Administration Manager
Andrea Fust
Accounts Assistant
Cherry Enriquez
Administrator Enrico Maullon
Driver Rafi Jamal

IT
IT Administrator Ajay Krishnan R.
Software Engineer Roshni Ahuja